pots in the garden

pots in the garden

expert design and planting techniques

RAY ROGERS

photographs by RICHARD HARTLAGE

TIMBER PRESS

contents

introduction:
pots in your garden

LET'S FACE IT: many of us have a rather limited space in which to garden, and most of us do not have all day to spend outside pursuing our hobby. Understandably, we want to use that precious space and our valuable time to their fullest potential. One of the most space-saving and time-efficient ways to enjoy our gardens is to include container plantings in our efforts. Container plantings do not need to take up much room (although they can fill your entire garden if you like), and a well-planned container, or a group of them, can be easily maintained in a surprisingly short amount of time.

Container gardening not only makes smart use of your space and good use of your time, but it is also as satisfying as gardening in the open ground. Not only can you grow many of the same plants that thrive in your beds and borders, but you also have the flexibility to move the plants around easily if you, or they, are not happy with the original spot. Additionally, container planting allows you to avoid transplanting, which can be hard on your plants, and using containers gives you more control over the specific soil, water, light, and other conditions your plants need to thrive. With container growing you are not bound by a plant's size in the same way you are with ground planting. You can elevate a low-growing plant to eye level or above or bring a tall plant down to eye level or below. You can cover up walls and railings with plants and fill window boxes to add to the appeal of your yard, deck, or porch.

Indeed, one of the most attractive aspects of container gardening is its malleability. If a plant or a combination of plants is not working for you, you can replace it with something that does. If that new terra-cotta pot does not quite suit your current plant selections, no problem: just swap it for a gray or green pot that does. Mix and match, trial and error, and wait (or not) and see: all of these techniques apply to gardening in general and to container growing in particular.

These are some of the classic arguments made for container gardening. Yet, it is my belief that not only is container gardening a time and space saver, it can easily be a preferred method of gardening, no matter the size of your garden. Also, just as inground gardening can be taken to the next level by applying various elements of design, so can container gardening be enhanced by considering these same elements. In these pages I discuss basic design elements, including color, line, form and mass, space, and texture, and I explore such topics as creating focal points, using empty containers, and bringing it all together in your overall garden design. I have also included essential and practical information on growing plants in containers and have examined the pros and cons of using all major plant groups, including annuals and perennials, trees and shrubs, cacti and other succulents, tropicals, bulbs, climbers and

trailers, and aquatics. Throughout the book, Richard Hartlage's superb photographs illustrate my points beautifully and will no doubt provide plenty of inspiration for your own gardening adventures.

Don't worry, though: you won't need a master of fine arts or a degree in horticulture to understand this book. What follows are one long-time gardener's accumulated thoughts on, and experiences with, container gardening, horticulture in general, and the basic principles behind good garden design. Neophytes and seasoned gardeners alike should find plenty of inspiration and instruction within these pages.

As you read this book, think about how you can adapt the design elements, the illustrated planting combinations, and the cultural information for your own garden. Imitation may be the highest form of flattery to some, but not to me: you'll pay me the greatest compliment by using my words and Richard's pictures as inspiration for your own container creations.

part i:
the elements of design

1: color

Color is arguably the most important element in container plantings and in gardening overall. It is also a good starting point when thinking about designing a container planting. Bright or subdued, analogous or contrasting, the colors chosen for a container planting (including the pot itself) all interact with each other in important ways. Whether those colors "work" is entirely up to the creator, as well as

the viewer, although some guidelines do exist to prevent you from making commonly agreed-upon mistakes.

Color may well be the most subjective of all the design elements;

think of how often you have heard someone express a strong reaction (negative or positive) to orange or magenta or bright red, as compared to their response to line or form or texture. It is no secret that color also elicits certain feelings and emotions, sometimes incongruous. Red may bring out a bit of aggression or at the very least suggest activity. Orange repels some and draws others to its autumnal warmth. Yellow is often seen as happy and friendly. Green can put people at ease, implying abundance and life, or bore them with its ubiquity. Blue generally cools things off, but it might also bring to mind clear summer skies. Purple often suggests nobility or sumptuousness. White is usually viewed as pure and all-inclusive, while black may be considered either sinister and foreboding or simple and elegant. Pink feels springlike and girlish, while brown conjures the mess of mud or the aroma and taste of chocolate cake. While you might disagree with these associations, you will probably admit that color has the power to elicit very personal reactions, both conscious and subconscious.

Many volumes have been written on color theory, and everyone who works, even occasionally, with color will no doubt have strong opinions on the subject. What follows is a basic introduction to using color. You are heartily encouraged to explore this endless subject well beyond this brief foray.

SIMPLE COLOR COMBINATIONS

Perhaps the easiest way to use color in a container planting is to place one strong color within a larger area of another equally strong or less robust one. The obvious contrast you create will immediately call attention to the planting and produce a focal point.

Bright orange-red Rieger begonias (*Begonia xhiemalis*) ❶ stand out simply yet dramatically against the various shades of green in this garden setting. Any bright color—including a vibrant green—would command attention in this context. Note how the black container almost disappears against the dark background, allowing the begonias to take center stage.

The principal color of a container planting does not necessarily need to be strong to make a statement: even subtle or muted colors will dominate when set within or against a compatible, essentially uniform "frame." Whether light, dark, or in between, the frame should create a pleasing contrast with the plant and container color(s).

No one would suggest that the colors of this *Solenostemon* (*Coleus*) 'Kiwi Fern' are bright and vibrant, but virtually everyone would agree that the "framing" blue of the bench ❷ contrasts sharply with the red and beige coloration of the plant and the earthy terra-cotta shades of the pot.

It is often not possible or practical to feature a single color within a relatively uniform area of another background color. However, if two or more surrounding or background colors seem visually "quiet," such as white, black, gray, or most darker colors, the entire combination will appear harmonious instead of disorganized.

Even though this purple-leaved Persian shield (*Strobilanthes dyerianus*) is set within a nonuniform background, ❸ the container planting stands out and the entire composition remains effective because of the less assertive nature of the white, gray, and green frame.

MORE-COMPLICATED COLOR COMBINATIONS

Combining two or more expressions of essentially the same color usually produces a pleasing, "safe" combination. The fun begins when one of the expressions differs in a dramatic way from its companions (such as a bright yellow flower set against a mass of cream-colored ones), or when the presence of the same color is not immediately obvious (as with many light and dark shades containing green, such as aqua, forest green, and chartreuse).

Different expressions of orange—one in the daisylike

Arctotis 'Pumpkin Pie' and others in the neighboring *Phygelius*—work together to produce a richly diverse yet unified presentation ❹. Note that most of the surrounding color is provided by shades of green; the bits of blue add a little contrast and give further life to the predominant oranges.

Rather than serving as the background for another color, green functions here ❺ as the dominant color among the containers, the plants, and the background, producing a subtle yet rich presentation. The many shades of green—ranging from dark purple-green to blue-green and plainer green to bright yellow-green—give this combination visual interest. The bright yellow-green adds some zing to what otherwise might be considered a rather muted or even somber collection of colors. Put your hand over the yellow-green to see for yourself.

Alternately, two colors that may not seem related on first glance can, on further inspection, reveal a happy, compatible connection. Combining the two colors with a more subtle third color produces a pleasing trio as well.

The dark *Solenostemon* (*Coleus*) 'Black Trailer' and the much lighter fanflower (*Scaevola aemula* 'Blue Fan') may not seem to be related in color at first glance, but closer inspection ❻ reveals that they are respectively very dark and rather light versions of purple. The greens of the fanflower leaves and the finely dotted edges of the coleus foliage tie in nicely with the related shades of the *Farfugium japonicum* 'Aureomaculatum' in the background and the ivy and other plants below the container.

A less obvious occurrence of the same basic color or colors can produce an almost subliminal expression of unity. You might not see the connec-

green, and blue-green. Including at least two members of a harmony in a container planting often produces a very pleasing combination, even more so when the setting for the container planting includes harmonious colors as well.

The very simple container planting ❽ of golden Baby Tears' yellow-green foliage (*Soleirolia soleirolii* 'Aurea') placed on the pedestal harmonizes beautifully with the

tion immediately, but the similarity is there if you look for it. Sometimes the more subtle color relationships produce the most satisfying results in container design.

Although the three coleus ('Big Red', 'Max Leuering', and 'India Frills') may initially seem widely (even jarringly) different from each other, a closer inspection ❼ yields the surprising discovery that all three are variations on the same basic theme of red and yellow-green.

HARMONIES

In color theory, two or more closely related colors are called "analogous harmonies." For example, red, orange, and yellow make a harmonious group, as do yellow-green,

even discord. At their best, though, contrasts make exciting additions to container plantings.

Sitting exactly opposite each other on the color wheel because they have no color in common, yellow and purple contrast strongly with each other to produce a combination full of visual energy. Adding to the impact here 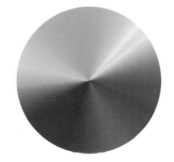 is the adventuresome use of richly colored spring-blooming flowers—daffodils (*Narcissus* 'Hawera') and violas—against a very dark, almost ominous, background of *Cordyline australis* 'Atropurpurea'. A more conventional and predictable planting would combine lighter

related blue-green of the ivy in this serene spot. Adding more blue or even purple would increase the harmonious effect, while throwing in bright red or orange would produce a strong and perhaps unattractive contrast.

Just a bit of contrast within a group of harmonious colors can provide a big kick to a container planting. The grouping shown here ⑨ combines many harmonious shades of green, with a coleus providing some contrasting—and refreshing—red. The solitary orange canna (*Canna* 'Pretoria') shines like a bright star in a much darker sky.

COMPLEMENTARY COLORS

According to color theory, combining colors that are considered opposite each other on the color wheel (called "complements;" see illustration below) produces a strong contrast. Instead of suggesting a peaceful sensation of rest and tranquility, contrasting colors can arouse feelings of unrest and

shades of yellow and purple with equally "springy" greens, but the designer of this planting turned the use of conventional spring colors on its ear.

Combining three colors spaced equidistantly from each other around the color wheel produces what is known as a triad. Red, blue, and yellow, or orange, violet, and green are common examples. You can give a container planting an air of sophisticated flair by employing a triad, but remember to show some restraint: adding too many colors to a container featuring a triad may result in a hodgepodge,

especially if the colors are all bright and saturated.

Yellow-green and orange-red, two of the three colors in a complementary triad, produce a striking contrast. If the glaze of the brighter blue pot on the right ⑪ contained a little more red (making it blue-purple), it would create a nearly perfect triad with the colors of the plants within. Nonetheless, the light blue contrasts nicely with the other colors because all three are quite bright. Cover up the bright blue pot to see how the darker one on the left does not play nearly as well with the brighter colors.

OTHER CONTRASTS

Colors set against each other, such as two closely related ones combined with one opposite them on the color wheel, often produce widely different yet pleasing contrasts in container plantings. Whether subtle or striking, such color combinations in the hands of a clever designer often produce a gratifying effect. Of course, since color perception is highly subjective, one designer's pleasing combination may be another's nightmare.

This combination ⑫ of red-orange, yellow, and blue comes quite close to composing the complementary (and often harmonious) triad of red, yellow, and blue, but there is some visual tension here. The brightness of all three colors turns up the energy. Also, placing the unrelated blue between the more closely related red-orange and yellow (instead of placing the blue to one side of the other two colors) adds to the excitement. Does this catch your eye, or do you find it clashing and abhorrent?

As subtle as the combination in the previous image is assertive, this grouping of plants ⑬ within its setting also demonstrates the idea of contrast. Alone in a mass of mostly gray and white, the richly colored and patterned coleus ('Japanese Giant') stands out against its companions (*Senecio viravira* and *Picea glauca* 'Conica'). No bright color catches your eye here, but a contrast exists nonetheless. As with the previous combination, beauty is in the eye of the beholder: you might consider this sophisticated and quietly stimulating, or maybe you find it uninspired and sleep-inducing.

POT COLORS

Don't forget to consider the color and style of your pots when putting together an interesting container planting. Pots often play an important part in the success or failure of a color combination and sometimes even take the lead, especially when a container's color stands in sharp contrast to the rest of the composition.

Various expressions ⑭ of red in the leaves of the coleus and the flowers of the fuchsia (*Fuchsia* 'Gartenmeister Bonstedt') make a noticeable, though not sharp, contrast with the yellow and chartreuse coleus foliage and *Helichrysum petiolare*. In turn,

virtually all of the plant colors, including that of the *Uncinia rubra* at the bottom, combine harmoniously with the brown and terra-cotta-colored pots. Only the white flowers of the *Hosta plantaginea grandiflora* seem a bit discordant. So how might a savvy designer take this composition to an even more interesting level?

With one simple, bold stroke the designer created a powerful contrast by placing a bright blue pot in front of all the other objects in the group. Since the blue does not echo any other color, it stands out vividly and makes the pot the center of attention. A more conservative designer might

have used a much darker blue pot (or may not have wanted to introduce any contrast), producing a "safer," more predictable color combination. But why be safe? Don't be afraid to use light- and bright-colored pots. However, keep in mind that such pots are probably best viewed as a visual snack of sorts and not as the eye's main course; too many variously colored pots will distract from the plants and the rest of the garden.

Instead of standing out, the color of a container can of course be worked in with the rest of the composition. Pots in darker shades of brown and terra-cotta look almost like soil, so they combine naturally with most

plant colors, as do dark green and black ones. Adventuresome designers go one step further by partnering unconventionally colored pots (such as apricot- or turquoise-colored ones) with matching and/or contrastingly colored plants.

Gentle blue-green pots, while not a conventional, "safe" color, interact attractively with their plants. The *Convolvulus cneorum* in the front container ⑮ is a lighter shade of the pot color, creating an easygoing change in brightness. On the other hand, the red-violet and pink ornamental cabbages in the back present strong contrasts. Notice where the two colors sit on the color wheel relative to blue-green: red-violet contains some blue and is within the same analogous harmony as blue-green, while pink (light red) has nothing in common with the blue-green. On closer inspection, the dark orange color of the rim completes a surprising triadic harmony with the red-violet cabbages and the blue-green pot. Whether you like one, or both (or neither!) of the cabbage colors with the pot, you must admit the combination is creative and adventuresome.

THE PEACEMAKERS

Sometimes you want to keep the things you love, such as children or favorite colors, close (but not too close) to each other. In container plantings, some colors are very useful for keeping the peace and separating certain favored hues. White, light to medium gray, pale yellow, and light

greenish yellow are examples of these peacekeepers. Placing one of these colors between two less-than-harmonious colors can create enough separation to make the combination work.

White can broker a truce between two colors that might not otherwise play together nicely. In this grouping ⑯ (see previous page), the white asters (*Aster pilosus* var. *pringlei* 'Monte Cassino') separate the purple asters and the golden rudbeckia, making the combination appear less antagonistic. However, be careful when using a very stark, bright white as a peacemaker, because too much of it can be as unsettling as two warring colors placed closely together.

Gray-leaved plants and pots ⑰ tend to work better as

peacemakers than bright white flowers or containers. Not only do leaves last longer than flowers, but gray is gentler on the eye than a cluster of white, especially in the strong sunlight of late spring and summer. Even though the two dusty millers (*Centaurea gymnocarpa*) are not placed between the brightly colored blooms of the *Verbena bonariensis* behind them, their grayness creates a visual distraction that separates the colors from each other, if only a little.

BE ADVENTURESOME

While you may already be armed with plenty of color-theory knowledge and personal experience, be open to the joys of experimentation and serendipity. Look carefully; you actually can find various incarnations of all three primary colors (red, blue, and yellow) as well as the three secondary colors (green, purple, and orange) present in a variety of plants. Using many different colors in combination may not be your cup of tea, but an argument can be made that a predominant blue/green/yellow harmony, for instance, with accents provided by a red-violet/red/red-orange harmony can create a plant combination that commands attention.

Bright red-orange tulips and dark red-violet leaves of *Bergenia* 'Bressingham Ruby' are the surprisingly harmonious players of this composition ⑱. Yellow-twig dogwood (*Cornus sericea* 'Flaviramea') branches pick up the tulip accent color, and everything is set off by the contrasting blue-greens of the tulip and Algerian ivy (*Hedera canariensis* 'Gloire de Marengo') foliage as well as the gray container. Whether composed by a master colorist or simply the result of happy coincidence, this is a visually stimulating composition worthy of emulation.

2: line and repetition

Line ranks closely behind color as one of the most immediately and readily perceived elements of design. Lines "move" visually to guide the viewer's eyes, whether strongly and straightforwardly from point A to point B, or in a gentler, less direct way, such as in an arc, bell curve, or sinuous, S-shaped Hogarthian curve. Other more complicated lines, such as a looping or zigzagging one, carry a great deal of visual energy, as do orderly multiples of the same basic line, such as a fan shape, starburst pattern, or the rails of train tracks as they seem to meet and then vanish in the distance. When two or more kinds of line interact, the result can be exciting, such as in a flower arrangement that deliberately combines a group of flowing lines with a group of straight ones, or confusing and weak, as when the various lines are disorganized and scattered. The latter is easily demonstrated by viewing a pile of sticks that were tossed and allowed to fall randomly.

Lines also define shapes, whether regular, as in circles and triangles,

or irregular, as in the outlines of many plants or sculptures (see Chapter 3 for a discussion of three-dimensional shapes). Conversely, shapes can create lines, as in a dotted line or when three or more pots are lined up along the edge of a patio or path, at the top of a wall, or running along one or both sides of a staircase. In each instance, whether essentially two-dimensional, such as the trunk of a tree, or distinctly three-dimensional, as in the row of upright parts of a pergola, a line leads your eye somewhere and can be used to create pleasing or perhaps visually disruptive garden scenes.

In container gardening, lines are encountered mostly as multiples, such as the upright stems of a shrub or the leaves of an ornamental grass emerging from a pot. Whether occurring as a small number of distinct lines or as a large group, if the lines all point in the same direction they present an almost irresistible stimulus for the viewer's eye to move toward a definite spot.

Even though the small side twigs present a slight distraction, the straight, upright shoots of the yellow-stemmed dogwood direct attention between the gray container ❶ and the dark green conifer above. The stems may appear to lead the eye upward or downward, depending on the viewer, but you cannot overlook the strong vertical action of the dogwood. Note the secondary vertical contributions made by the foliage of the double-flowered hyacinth (*Hyacinthus* 'Hollyhock'), the white pillar, and the ivy-clad tree trunk. Subtler yet still playing important parts are the briefly interrupted vertical lines of the gray pot and the gently curving line of the variegated Algerian ivy to the right side of it.

Do you have any doubt where to look here ❷? The clearly vertical lines of the red-edged *Libertia peregrinans* compel the viewer to look up and down between the clay pot and the juniper in the background before moving along to the chartreuse and soft-gray foliage on either side. Imagine how a horizontally branched shrub or an arching mass of stems would lead the eye in a very different direction.

In nature, of course, lines are not always thin, but even a thick or massive line implies movement. The trunk of a giant redwood certainly compels an observer's eyes to move from the ground to the sky and back again, while the substantial "trunks" of a potted banana tree or the massive column of a Greek temple illustrate the same visual principle.

Your initial reaction to a stout-stemmed Madagascar palm (*Pachypodium lamerei*) may not be the same as a slender, colored twig shrub or grasslike perennial ❸, but all three

create the impression of up-and-down movement in the end. The eye inevitably ends up at the tufts of leaves via a linear pathway from the pots. Take note of how the leaf tufts appear to convert the energy of a single line of movement into a smaller burst of motion, much as the fiery single trails of fireworks turn into clusters of dynamic lines.

Lines need not always create a feeling of direct, straight-line movement. You can have a little fun with a line by making it move in a spiral. Your eye still proceeds from point A to point B; it just takes a little more time to get there.

Here ❹ is a literal and figurative twist on a standard bay (*Laurus nobilis*) topiary: instead of a ramrod-straight stem leading the eye between the pot and the head of foliage, an open spiral takes the eye on a slower but more visually engaging path. An even more open spiral might look accidental and lazy, while a much tighter spiral (one with more turns) might lose its linear quality and look more like a thick trunk.

Lines arching outward from a central point—creating a fanlike

shape—guide a viewer's gaze almost as effectively as straight ones do. Even though such lines do not proceed from one narrowly perceived point or area to another, they nonetheless repeatedly take the eye from the starting point to one destination, then back to the starting point, and finally on to another destination. This detailed journey provides for a more engaging and interesting experience than one that goes simply and exclusively from point A to point B.

The arching red *Phormium* 'Guardsman' provides an eye-catching journey ❺ against an otherwise

less engaging backdrop of green foliage. The strong fan shape also steals some of the thunder from the bright *Geum* 'Red Wings', whose vivid but spotty color fails to provide as much interest as the strongly linear, but less colorful, phormium. Also note the two plants at the base of the phormium; both the intricate starburst shape of the blue-green *Puya coerulea* and the simpler, upright leaves of the linearly variegated *Agave americana* 'Mediopicta' play secondary but still significant directional roles in this composition. Notice how the dark color and horizontal lines of the pot add a breath of contrast.

The course of a line is not always as immediately apparent as in the preceding examples, where your eye is obviously meant to move singly or repeatedly from one place

to another. If you want to create a more subtle feeling of movement, use plants that are not as strongly and immediately perceived as linear. The directional effect will still be present but on a less obvious, almost subliminal level.

Although the plant in this container ⑥ conveys more a feeling of solid mass than line, a closer look reveals many vertical stems among the leaves. Of added interest is the more obvious horizontal presence created by the leaves of the yellow loosestrife (*Lysimachia punctata* 'Alexander'), the bands of the blue and yellow flowers below the main plant, and the painted bands at the top of the column. Uncovering this less apparent vertical movement within the horizontal elements creates an exciting sense of discovery for the viewer. Note how the lines of the plants in both the upper-right and lower-right corners add to the subtle, vertical visual action.

Up to now we have chiefly considered the vertical, horizontal, and arching movements suggested by a straight or singly curved line or lines. A group of lines can also appear to move inward or outward from a central point, producing a starburst pattern, such as the *Dyckia* at left in . The many lines contained within such a pattern suggest explosive (or implosive) energy.

DON'T FORGET THE POTS

Many containers can charitably be described as plain or hardworking, such as simple and widely used terra-cotta pots. However, as with color, line can play a vital and absorbing role when you are choosing which pots to combine with which plants and with other pots.

While most people would likely be drawn first to the colors and shapes of the plants ❼ as well as the pots shown here, who could fail to notice the vertical lines of the three larger containers? Just as stems and leaves draw the eye up and down in the previous examples, so do the ridges on these pots. Note how the creator of this combination chose to continue the lines in two of the pots with the outward- and downward-radiating starbursts of the *Dyckia* on the left and the upward-reaching *Sempervivum* on the right. Use your imagination to picture what might be planted in the

Neither the color nor the shape of this pot ⑧ grabs your attention as in the previous image, yet an intriguing interplay of lines nevertheless occurs. The rustic twiglike ornamentation of the otherwise plain terra-cotta lends interest by itself, but a closer look reveals how the leaves, flowers, and stems of the *Begonia boliviensis* echo the intersecting lines on the pot: their linear qualities and occasionally overlapping parts suggest the crossing lines of the container. Some may argue that the mundane (or perhaps uncomplementary) color of the pot unfavorably trumps any other attractive attribute, while others may look beyond the pot's color to appreciate the subtle line play.

LINES CAN BE ROUND, TOO

Connecting a line with itself in a radially symmetrical fashion produces a circle. And circles occur everywhere in gardening: flowers, leaves, fruits, pots, patio tiles, furniture, and other garden elements display circular outlines or other radial attributes. In contrast to open lines, which elicit active feelings of motion and energy, circles suggest the passive qualities of repose and rest, of stability, quietude, and contentment. In container gardening, pots with circular rims present a restful frame for the plants within them, at least when viewed from above or at an angle that preserves the feeling of the circle.

Circles abound in this composition—from the pot rims to the rounded silhouettes of the rosettes of many of the succulent plants ⑨ (among them echeverias and sedums) to even the seat of the chair. Only the flowering stems of the succulents, some of their upward-reaching leaves, and the chair legs challenge the dominance of the circles in

tallest container at the back—is it a vertically oriented plant to continue the basic line of the ensemble in the forefront, or perhaps one with arching or starburstlike lines to direct the viewer's eye outward or downward to contain the group visually? Also note how the dense, rounded, almost static form of the *Echeveria* at the bottom strongly contrasts with its much more linear and more energetic companions, as does the plain, unlined pot. Is the echeveria the odd one out, or is it in fact the focal point?

this composition. The curved lines surrounding the chair's seat add a bit of gentle variety and lead the eye upward, preventing the entire composition from looking hunched down.

REPETITION

Connect two or more points or objects in a row and what do you get? A line. Whether you literally draw a line between the items or fill it in with your mind's eye, repeating a few or more items creates the image or impression of a line. Since you probably do not want to draw actual lines in your garden, you can take advan-

tage of the energy that they suggest by arranging containers (or garden objects, pillars, or whatever works for you) in some linear manner. This visual impression of a line will achieve the same basic result as the more straightforward lines discussed previously in this chapter—the viewer's eye will follow it—but the impact can be much greater because of the increased complexity of the objects that create the line.

Three specimens of *Agave americana* 'Marginata' in a row  make a line to guide the eye—and the feet—to the next level of this terraced

garden. Note how the carefully aligned, square-sided pots with their sharp 90-degree angles aid in producing the illusion of a line. Carefully arranged rounded or conical pots would also create the impression of a straight line, though less strongly, whereas rectangular pots would do the job even more effectively. You could make a much more literal line by joining rectangular pots end to end, but that would leave nothing to the viewer's imagination. Great art, which includes great landscaping, compels the observer to fill in the missing parts of a picture or scene.

Once your eye moves from the large, white umbrella in this scene ⑪ from the Hardie Garden in Nutley, New Jersey, it should follow the line created by the row of now four specimens of *Agave americana* 'Mediopicta' along the edge of the patio. Although the pots are not square-sided as in the previous picture, readily suggesting a line, the use of four items instead of three helps strengthen the linear illusion. Not only do the four plants in their pots suggest linearity, but they also produce a line expanded to three dimensions: a plane. In this case

(11)

the plane plays the role that a wall or hedge might elsewhere, but with very practical attributes: flexibility and portability. You can make a "hedge" of pots as long as you want, move it around to fine-tune its appearance, or even carry it to another part of the garden for reassembly.

At first glance ⑫ a viewer might find nothing remarkable in a paved area bordered by a row of 'Spring Green' tulips, but in this case the paved area and the space above it is defined—not simply edged—by a screen of tall tulips in oversized pots. A few days after this picture was taken the tulips faded, but a creative

designer might well have come along and replaced the tulips with tall-growing annuals. A row of container-grown shrubs or topiaries would also maintain the impression of a screen.

Sometimes a line is best expressed subtly, just as color or any other design element might be used in a low-key way. For example, an area lacking uniformity or cohesion benefits greatly from an assertive line placed along one or more sides. Think of the buttoned-down look a precisely cut edge or row of Belgium block creates along a lawn, or how a neatly clipped hedge or low stone wall defines the

bed or walkway next to it. Although the lines of the previous examples are readily visible, their simplicity makes them subtle—as does a row of pots set within a bed or other planting instead of placed alongside it.

The planting in the foreground ⑬ appears very informal. However, the placement of the four blue pots and their plants diverts the eye and ties the area together, serving both as a unifying hedge or wall behind the planting and as a directional line guiding the eye to the bench in the background. Although the bright orange-red flowers of the *Pelargonium*

cannot be described as subtle, the placement of the pots within the planting, instead of at the edge, can be considered subtly creative.

All of the elements in a line do not need to be identical (or nearly so) to create a linear impression. As long as the elements are not wildly dissimilar and there are enough of them in a row, they produce nearly as immediate and strong a line as one formed by very similar or identical objects. In fact, such variation may even appear more visually interesting once the observer takes the time to inspect the individual components of the line.

Borrowing from the railroad-track principle mentioned in the introduction to this chapter, Roberto Burle Marx left no doubt where to look first ⑭ at his private residence. Even the heads of the animal sculptures seem to be looking in the same direction! Notice the row of containers and plants placed along the wall; while all of the containers are basically bowl-shaped and all of the plants could be described as vaselike, the subtle differences between the containers and the plants add a great deal of visual interest. After taking in the long view, who would not want to move along this space to admire each plant and pot.

NONLINEAR REPETITION

Of course, repetition in garden design is not confined exclusively to linear arrangements. While a series of lines can unify a scene or even elicit powerful emotions (picture the vertical bars of a prison cell or the seemingly endless row of tombstones in the cemetery at the site of the D-day Normandy invasion), repeating other design elements can likewise tie a garden together.

Arching and feathery shapes (all produced by clustered lines), as well as colors, occur repeatedly in this setting ⑮ at Ganna Walska Lotusland, producing a unified whole. The lines of the potted *Astelia chathamica* 'Silver Spear' echo those of the *Agapanthus* in the ground, while the nearly continuous swath of palms in the background repeat the arch motif. The blue tone of the *Astelia* on either side of the pond further ties the scene together, as does the terra-cotta color of the pots and the pavers. Even the sides of the bench get into the act by picking up the color of the gray concrete. The red-leaved purple sugarcane (*Saccharum officinarum* 'Pele's Smoke') on the extreme left side and the large tree trunk stand out as the mavericks in this composition, providing a welcome bit of contrast.

A strong repetition of line exists here **16** in the concentric circles of the brick edging, the bluestone, and in the circular outline of the container planting. Using a single flower color would produce an even stronger feeling of repetition, but the designer chose to have some fun with the three colors while still retaining the theme of the three concentric circles.

How can you bring some visual order to a widely divergent group of plants? Grow them in a series of similar (or identical, if you choose) containers.

Virtually every plant in this grouping  (see previous page), although widely different in color and habit, thrives in a gray concrete container. The white topdressing on the surface of many of the pots provides a bit more unity. The careful observer will also note how the rectangular, gray paving stones echo both the shape and color of the containers. Notice how the designer avoided monotony by varying the sizes, shapes, and placement of the pots. .

Serendipity—or sometimes clever, careful placement and planning—always makes for memorable results, whether in gardening or any other human pursuit. Part of the fun of gardening springs from observing these happy occurrences in your yard, or elsewhere, and then sharing the experience with others.

Agave americana 'Mediopicta' makes a fine container plant for many settings, provided it receives plenty of sun and space to spread its dramatically arching and patterned leaves. For whatever reason, the gardener placed a birdcage next to the agave ⑱, perhaps because the spot accommodated both items conveniently.

No doubt the gardener was pleasantly surprised to see the additional elements created by the dramatic shadows of the setting sun. At first glance the agave appears to be inside a cage, but a second look reveals the reality of the placement. Need it be pointed out that the straight lines of the cage and its straight and curved shadows contrast attractively with the straight and curved lines of the pot and plant, respectively? Even more dramatic is the plant's shadow that almost perfectly echoes the form of the plant, conjuring images of an octopus or an imagined alien lifeform.

18

3: form and mass

The element of form logically follows line in container-gardening design. In the most basic terms, the form or shape of a two-dimensional figure, such as a circle or rectangle, or a three-dimensional one, such as a sphere or a cone, is determined by one or more lines. A trip back to geometry class provides examples of how lines create three-dimensional objects: an infinite number of equal-length lines radiating from a central point define a sphere, and a line drawn from a point and moving along the circumference of a circle generates a cone. Since pure geometric shapes rarely occur in gardening—except as man-made containers and other manufactured objects—this chapter necessarily deals with more organic, and therefore less regular and perfect, shapes. However, some of these forms can, with human intervention, come quite close to perfect geometric shapes. The arts of topiary and frame-training, which combine horticulture with geometry, allow the designer to use rather precise shapes to make garden statements.

Mass (or bulk), for our purposes, will be considered in terms of perceived density and weightiness. A large, uncut boulder or a legless, overstuffed couch appears solid and dense, whereas an extensively chiseled sculpture incorporating a lot of holes or an uncovered wire-frame garden chair appears far less heavy. The more visible the space or spaces contained within an object, the less massive the object seems.

Both the form and mass of a plant play major, though often unassertive and sometimes subliminal, roles in its overall appearance. A plant's form may appear linear, arch-ing, drooping, spreading, or globular, while its mass may come across as thick and solid or open and light. Although not usually perceived as quickly as color, form and mass are often more lastingly important in the overall presentation of a container planting, both immediately and over the entire growing season. While not as immediately gratifying to work with as color, form and mass comprise the backbone of a planting.

Form and mass carry symbolism for (and elicit emotional responses from) people just as color does. The gender perceptions inspired by form and mass, whether considered stereotypical or not, are obvious examples. As with color, however, the same shape will connote something very different or very similar to two different people. For example, a large, solid sphere may feel male to some because of its solidity and stability, while another might deem the sphere female, owing to its round, soft outline. Similarly, a thick, relatively short obelisk or cone might suggest masculinity for obvious phallic reasons to one person, while a tall, thin obelisk or delicate wire-frame topiary cone might readily be described as feminine by another. And some people might not perceive any gender-suggestive signals from objects or plants in general, or in particular.

Of course, gender associations are not the only example of our emotional or subliminal reactions to form and mass. Circles and spheres, since they contain no visible line that seems to move from point A to point B (the outline moves from A to A instead), can evoke feelings of self-containment, perfection, and stability. Design-oriented garden-ers use spheres (or close approximations of them), such as rounded topiaries, hanging baskets, globelike containers, and even bowling balls and gazing balls, to elicit such feelings from the observer.

Combining spheres with lines and other forms can produce more visual interest as well. Although the sphere may be the dominant shape in a composition, adding simple lines, as well as rectangles and other angular forms, keeps the eye moving, providing apparent motion and added visual appeal. Adding one or more smaller spheres or circular shapes—thus exploiting the power of repeti-tion—will increase the impact of the dominant sphere.

The designer of this setting ❶ reduced the composition to almost pure geometric forms. The larger, lower topiary ball of boxwood (*Buxus sempervirens*) sits placidly on the cubelike container, while the smaller one seems to float above both. Three circular fountainheads obviously echo the rounded topiary heads, while the balls bobbing in the pool subtly and very cleverly continue the spherical theme. Also note how the squared-off shape of the wall repeats the form of the container.

composition can produce two very different impressions, depending on the space that exists between the forms. The perception of space between forms allows the shapes to present themselves individually and also encourages the eye to move from one object to another, creating action in the composition. However, if little or no detectable space appears between the individual shapes, a dense, amorphous blob usually results, providing neither the suggestion of a specific form nor the feeling of movement.

If a circle or sphere seems complete and at rest, what feeling does a half circle or half sphere (let's call it a mound) suggest? Some offer that a mound connotes the stability and containment of an arch or dome, while others contend it represents irregular motion (moving from a curved line to a straight one along the outline) and separation, as if the other half of the sphere had been removed.

Ajania pacifica naturally grows as a well-formed mound, allowing a garden designer to utilize the plant's shape ❷ without much sculptural intervention (clipping and other training). Note how the golden flower clusters make the mound look less dense than if it were all green. Repetition plays a part here, both in the obvious use of two mounds of *A. pacifica* as well as the darker, denser mound of dwarf boxwood on the right. Placing three repeated shapes in the same area makes a stronger statement than using just one.

Using many occurrences of the same basic form in a

Most of the rounded forms in ❸—not all spherical nor made of the same materials—stand out even more from each other because of the space that exists between them. The potted oval *Cordyline australis* 'Albertii', the single silver sphere, and the pink-toned balls all exist distinctly from one another, so the eye moves easily between the cordyline and the metal spheres. Note that the silver spheres in the pot do not come across as individual pieces but instead as a solid mass. In contrast, ❹ shows two very attractive containers of *Aeonium arboreum* 'Zwartkop', though from a distance the individual circular rosettes appear to merge into a blob. While the color of the rosettes and their contrast with the containers and setting catch the eye, only a closer look reveals the fascinating rounded form of the individuals making up the whole.

Color can also be used to alter the perception of form or mass. For instance, if you think that a bright rounded form would stand out too much in a container planting, consider using the form in a dark color. It will still be there but in a more subtle way,

color forces them to play a secondary role to the fans of the pineapple lily, letting their arching leaves stand out. If the oxalis spheres were the same shade of green as the pineapple lily, the latter would be almost visually lost.

Let's move on to another expression of form: the cone. The outline (silhouette) of a cone brings two lines together in a point, doubly exploiting the directional nature of a single line. This shape and its visual power is most dramatically represented in gardens by giant conifers such as blue Colorado spruce (*Picea pungens* 'Glauca'), Douglas fir (*Pseudotsuga menziesii*), and the dwarf Alberta spruce (*Picea glauca* var. *albertiana* 'Conica'). A cone may also be created by carefully clipping a tree or shrub or training a climber onto a conical form.

Although conical conifers may, by virtue of their solid colors and considerable mass, imply a feeling of permanence, strength, and masculinity, multicolored and more open, less substantial cones project a more transient, softer, and feminine image. Both expressions can make strong garden statements.

There is a lot going on in this picture, but once the viewer's eyes move past the brightly colored plants in the foreground ❻ and the strong vertical lines of the background, a pleasant surprise appears: three cones hold this composition together. The obvious large cone in the foreground of black-eyed Susan vine (*Thunbergia alata*) projects strength through its size and mass, but the golden flowers and open space at the top lend a lighter, almost delicate touch. In the background, the very simple all-green cone and even more Spartan, stripped-down cone made by the joined upright poles complete the group of three, though the two

allowing other elements to assume greater importance in the composition.

At first glance, most people probably notice the bright yellow coleus and the blue wall ❺. The next look reveals the fanlike pineapple lily (*Eucomis* 'Sparkling Burgundy') in the center of the picture, and only then does the eye fall onto the dark purple spheres of massed oxalis (*Oxalis triangularis* ssp. *triangularis*) growing at the base of the fans. Although the oxalis spheres possess the strongest, most well-defined form in the composition, their dark

in the background project a far less
emphatic feeling than the dominant
foreground cone. Imagine how different this composition would appear if
all three cones were solid green or all
dotted with golden flowers (the cones
might well become the immediate
center of attention in spite of the
other colors and lines in the scene),
or if they were all merely cones made
of three poles lashed together (they
might well be lost among the lines of
the background).

Just as all spheres or rounded forms
are not solid masses with distinct
outlines (see the cordyline on page
42), neither must all cones appear
dense and precisely linear in outline.
Think of Charlie Brown's Christmas
tree or the spokes on the underside
of an opened umbrella. Open cones
still project the form and direction of
more substantial ones, yet their less
precise silhouette and greatly reduced
mass express the feeling more subtly.

Looking more like a quickly
drawn sketch than real plants, a
group of toothed lancewood (*Pseudo-
panax ferox*) at Heronswood Nursery
in Washington State ❼ (see next
page) nevertheless expresses a conical

spheres and cones (and other "pure" solids, including pyramids and prisms). However, they still present a distinctive appearance and can evoke feelings of movement or even suggest attributes of gender. Drawing as much on line as form, these shapes contribute significantly to dramatic garden scenes.

Fanlike *Agave americana* 'Marginata' creates a powerful impression ❽ through its combination of the contrasting outlines of a point-side-down cone and a mound. Whether the lines appear to go up (the cone) and down (the mound) or basically downward—or maybe even inward—depends on individual perception, but any of those scenarios implies movement. Although produced by only a small number of elements (the leaves), the strong, energetic form makes as much of an impression as a more massive spherical or conical topiary or a trained form composed of hundreds or thousands of leaves.

The outwardly radiating starburst form of the *Phormium* 'Maori Queen' consists of a great many lines ❾ that in outline suggest a circle or oval, expressing both movement and containment. It might even be argued that the linear leaves suggest the sound of rustling pompoms, clashing cymbals, or rushing water (see Chapter 9, Other Sensory Elements).

Turning briefly from form to mass, let's consider a couple of examples of mass modified by other design factors. A solid expanse of the same color or shape projects a feeling of greater density (mass) than does a more diverse presentation, which may offer more visual interest. Generally, the greater the number of diverse elements contained within an object or group, the less massive and

feeling. Instead of mass primarily expressing the form, line does most of the job here. Placing just one plant on the table would result in a more readily perceived cone shape, while grouping three of them provides more mass and therefore more to observe. Note how the pots, while lacking the point of a cone, creatively suggest a reverse image of the shapes above them. A square or rounded pot would fail to produce the subtle repetition of form.

Other popular garden forms, such as fans and starburst shapes, lack the clear outlines and greater apparent mass of

more engaging it will seem. Although a box of all-green marbles of the same size presents a unified and massive whole, a box of multicolored marbles of different sizes looks less dense and therefore less massive. However, both examples represent useful design approaches: a uniform, dense background (such as a hedge behind a multicolored herbaceous border) will tie together a complicated foreground, and one unique element can stand out dramatically from the crowd (such as one little topiary standing bravely among a group of much larger ones).

Look closely at the container at

the top of picture **10**. The uniformly blue-green foliage of the *Echeveria* presents a relatively massive appearance, but the orange flowers above divert the eye and lighten the look. The other two containers hold several different succulents; their various colors, shapes, and sizes create a less dense, massive feeling than would solid, uniform groups of the same kind of plant. The close-up **11** of the red-edged echeveria shows how both line and color can lessen the sense of mass: the wavy, complicated edges lighten the broad, thick leaves, and the red markings break up what would other-

wise be a solid expanse of green.

Even though the outline of the entire purple and white grouping ⑫ creates a large oval shape, inserting the purple asters among the white ones (*Aster pilosus* var. *pringlei* 'Monte Cassino') introduces diversity and breaks up what would otherwise be a solid, less visually engaging mass of white. Imagine if this group of asters were exclusively purple or white: the uniformity would suggest greater mass, regardless of the color.

Although a third or even fourth color would reduce the feeling of mass even further, it is wise to limit the number of diverse elements to prevent diluting the strength of the design element you intend to emphasize. As the saying goes, "Too many cooks spoil the broth."

CONSIDERING THE POT AND OTHER GARDEN ELEMENTS

As with color and line, the form and mass of a container can play an impor-

tant part in good design. A carefully chosen pot complements the plant(s) by presenting a striking contrast, by acting in subtle harmony, or by relating to the planting in any of a number of other ways.

An unusual plant deserves an equally distinctive container ⑬ (see next page). Both the colors and arguably bizarre linear and curvilinear forms of the pitcher plants (*Sarracenia purpurea* and *S. leucophylla*) contrast sharply but attractively with the gray rectangular container, bringing to mind a plinth or shelf used to display some sort of prized art object or natural artifact. A simple terra-cotta pot would make a mismatched companion for the eccentric pitcher plants, just as an elaborately ornamented, multicolored container would divert too much attention from these unique plant forms that demand to be seen (and heard, if you fancy the pitchers as trumpets).

Even a common plant can be carried to a higher esthetic level by choosing a somewhat complementary container. Most tulips cannot match pitcher plants in terms of rarity and distinctive form, but look how the

designer of this combination  knew how to maximize the potential of both the plants and the pot. Not only does the form of the container echo the shape of the individual flowers (*Tulipa* 'Artist'), but the pot color almost matches the foliage, and the blue-green of the pot exists in perfect and pleasing contrast to the red-orange of the flowers (see the color wheel illustration, page 17).

The form of a container-grown plant can relate to objects other than its pot as well. A creative designer considers the surrounding plants, surfaces, structures, and other ornaments when composing and placing a planted container or grouping. Here lies fertile ground for combin-

ing masterful horticulture with inspired design.

At first glance, no deliberate relationship seems to exist between the large sculpture and the pot of cannas (*Canna* 'Phaison') next to it . However, look closely at how the cannas' leaves appear in pairs at the top of each stem, resembling the paired broad "fingers" that emerge from the sculpture's elongated base. Also, the more open sculpture at the back presages the appearance of the cannas' informal flower clusters.

4: space and placement

Space may be considered the negative counterpoint to other positive design elements. It displays no color or mass, yet it plays an integral role in visual texture (different from surface texture) and closely interacts with line and form in defining the shape of objects. Like line, space is an element contained to some degree within individual plants and solitary container plantings and is also a factor in the interaction between two or more containers and their plants. Some people give space no conscious consideration during the creation of a container planting, but for the savvy designer it stands on equal footing with color, line, form, mass, and texture.

In order to understand the nature and benefits of space, let's first consider settings where space is not visually apparent and where this absence may interact unfavorably among objects. Think of space in terms of the breathing room around a plant and its container, as well as the distance that exists between two or

more plants, pots, and other objects near a container planting. Space allows an object to appear as something distinct from the rest of its surroundings. Without enough space an object may seem confined or partially obscured. On the other hand, some observers may find close proximity to be a pleasing aspect of a composition, suggesting abundance and fecundity. As with other design elements, there is a lot of room for subjectivity; nonetheless, a little awareness of the basic nature of such elements enables a designer to produce generally satisfying results.

Although the colors, lines, forms, and textures of these plants ❶ produce some satisfying combinations, it could be argued that a viewer might have difficulty perceiving the characteristics of the individual plants and their containers. It could also be argued that the entire composition lacks a sense of coherence, as no readily perceived feeling of direct movement exists. Try this mental exercise: Remove the grassy-leaved, blue-flowered *Agapanthus* in the middle of the composition. Its absence permits a direct view of the agave and its container, which for many viewers might be considered the most eye-catching member of this group. Removing the agapanthus also creates a central space around which the eye can move in an orderly fashion, enabling appreciation of each plant and pot individually.

For some, this composition ❷ might fail because it lacks space, but notice the railing. The diagonal of the railing leads the eye in a given direction, visually tying the composition together. Also, this composition runs up one side of a staircase, although the stairs are barely visible in the picture. The open space of the stairs borders one side of the grouping, creating a void (space) against which the

plants and their pots can stand out, as well as an irregular edge (line) that acts in almost the same directional manner as the railing. The designer provides a visual feast of colors, lines, forms, and textures, and it is up to the viewer to decide whether the lack of space detracts from the design or is instead compensated by the visual coherence provided by the railing and the placement along the open space of the staircase.

A single container planting can benefit from interacting with space as much as a grouping can. So how much space is enough? Is it always optimal for a container and its contents to be displayed with open space all around? There are no hard and fast rules for dealing with space when grouping plants; the same principle applies to individual pots and plants.

This container planting ❸ receives high marks for attractive color, visual movement, interesting form interplay, and textural variety. However, the close placement of the benches appears to confine the planting and deprives it of the elbow room necessary to display its full beauty. The benches also visually compete with the planting for attention. Several scenarios could be offered to remedy this situation: (1) raise the pot on a compatible plinth so that the base of the container is flush with the level of the seats; (2)

grow the plants in a taller pot that raises the planting to a pleasing level; (3) move the benches farther away from the planting; or (4) place the planting at the other side of one of the benches.

There is no doubt that, whether big or small or composed of one plant or many, a container planting assertively stands out when surrounded by plenty of space. Physically separating plantings from other objects, no

matter how visually distracting they may be, helps keep the eye focused on the planting.

Although large objects compete for attention here, the space around the king-sized container planting ❹ sets this plant apart—both physically and visually—from the rest of the scene. Of course, color plays a role in catching the eye, but even a bigger, more colorful planting would suffer if not given enough room; its colors and other attributes would compete with surrounding objects for attention.

The white patio furniture may attract your eye at first, but then the container planting in the foreground ❺ jumps out, partially because of the considerable amount of space around it. Yes, the appealing colors and forms of the succulents command attention as well, but not until the space around them directs the viewer's eye to the planting as a whole. Adding another container planting or object, or placing the succulents much closer to the patio furniture, would diminish the strong presence of the planting.

A solitary potted agave takes center stage ❻ (see next page) at the corner of this wall for several reasons. The terra-cotta color of the pot stands out from the predominant greens and grays of the wall, while the feeling of movement produced by the linear leaves attracts attention. However, it can also be argued that much of this container's visual impact derives from the plant being almost completely surrounded by space. Try to picture the plant in a very low pot hunched down among the ivy, and you will almost feel the reduction in the visual energy of this scene.

In the identical spot in the same garden as that shown in the previous image, but at another point in time and from a different camera angle, a different agave (*Agave*

americana 'Marginata')—an arguably visually stronger one—assumes a less dominant role in the overall composition ❼. The flowering clematis (*Clematis paniculata*) and dark green hydrangea (*Hydrangea anomala* ssp. *petiolaris*) physically and visually encroach on both the pot and the plant, which results in a lack of apparent space around the container, diminishing its presence. Admittedly, the vantage point from which the two agaves are viewed plays a role in their differing visual strengths: the first one is backed by a broad swath of green, whereas the second must compete for attention with the building and separate green masses in the background.

Is providing space (and a more

or less uniform background) around a plant and its pot the only way to feature a particularly attractive container planting? The decision ultimately rests with the designer, but as in so many other aspects of gardening, design, and life in general, there may be more than one way to achieve a pleasing result.

Which do you feel makes the more attractive setting for the *Caladium humboldtii*? Spatially isolating it on the gray table ❽ invites the viewer to admire the intricate patterns on the leaves and their apparent outward

movement almost exclusively; only after feasting the eyes on the caladium does attention move to the other objects. However, who can deny the appeal of the composition that combines the caladium with the equally enticing pig sculpture and the purple flowers of the hosta ❾? Although little feeling of space exists around the caladium, it still holds its visual ground with the other objects in the picture.

THE SPACE BETWEEN

A pair of nearly identical container plantings makes a strong statement no matter where the two pots sit relative to each other, yet the feeling created depends on the closeness of the pots. At its most basic, an adjacent or touching pair appears as one unit, while the individual pots in a separated duo clearly come across as distinct objects. A closer look might reveal an even more complex perception by an imaginative observer: an adjacent pair might evoke a feeling of unity or the opposite sensation of conflict, while the separated pair might suggest division or, alternatively, a feeling of coordinated action. On yet another level, the pair in close proximity might feel accidental, or casual and informal, whereas a separated pair could appear more deliberate and formal.

Do these two pots of crocuses ('Lady Killer' and 'Ruby Giant') ❿ suggest an easygoing attitude or a more formal, buttoned-down approach to design? Perhaps they suggest the harmony of a stable relationship, or maybe they look

like two armies on the verge of battle. Whatever the feeling produced, the close placement evokes emotions and images different from those that would be elicited by the same two pots placed farther apart. As always, other design elements come into play here: try to imagine the visual and emotional effects that would be created if one pot contained only purple crocuses and the other only white ones, or if just one purple crocus bloomed among a mass of white.

With more distance between them, these two pots of *Hakonechloa macra* 'Aureola'  should elicit different reactions than the two pots of crocuses. In any case, it is clear that there are two separate objects here; the impression is produced not only by the space between the two plants but also by the two circular tables that define the space under them. Although they are not identical standard topiaries (plants that would conventionally be used by many in this setting), the two rather shaggy-looking plants still create a symmetrical, formal feeling. How would that feeling change if both plants sat on the same table or if one were placed on the bricks? Not only does the amount of space between two similar objects play a role in design, but so too do their relative positions in space. Positioning objects on the same plane suggests agreement and formality, while placement on two separate planes implies difference and informality.

Two cordylines (*Cordyline australis* 'Albertii') and two pots of tulips (*Tulipa* 'Gaiety') spaced widely on

either side of a gravel path ⑫ present a very formal, deliberate appearance. Had all four pots been placed in a different arrangement—for instance, if the tulip pots both sat to the right of the cordylines or if both pots flanked one of the cordylines—the impression created would be quite different, suggesting deliberate informality or maybe implying a lack of careful thought.

Space does not only apply on a single plane, of course. A designer can highlight a container planting by placing it above the rest of the composition.

The potted agave plays the dominant role ⑬ (see next page), in spite of the many colors vying for attention in the border below it. The agave appears almost to float among the rest of the static members of the scene. Admittedly, its strong coloration and form also figure into the agave's assertiveness, but the plant's high perch leaves no doubt as to who is king of the hill. Even if the photographer had not positioned his camera to incorporate a flattering green background (the tree) for the agave, the pot would still command attention, partially because of its elevated

spot. The pot's color helps it stand out as well.

Thomas Hobbs of Vancouver, British Columbia, cleverly used elevation ⑭ to feature a colorful collection of succulents in an unconventional container. The rounded arch literally and visually lifts the plants into prominence, leaving no doubt as to where to look.

Window boxes have been used for centuries to lift a planting above the rest of a garden or other setting. Even a simply constructed window box displaying one kind of plant demands visual attention, but the example here

15 grabs the viewer by the eye and will not let go. Color, line, form, and elevation combine to make an exuberant and undeniably appealing composition.

This simple window box **10** increases the perception of visual movement by letting its contents cascade in a dramatic waterfall of foliage. Using more compact, self-contained plants in the box would produce an entirely different expression of movement (or perhaps no feeling of movement at all).

One might say that the container

planting **17** (see next page) assumes a subservient role to the tall, colorful column, which sends the plants and their pot into orbit above the earthbound flora below. Or does the planting play an integral part in making the overall combination of the column and pot the dominant feature of the scene? Put your fingers over the planting to get an idea of how the column's impact would change without the planting, and then try imagining the difference that a shorter column or a less colorful one might create.

HANGING CONTAINERS

Hanging a container is a logical means of exploiting the design power of space and appropriate placement. Thoughtfully situated, a hanging planting uses the space around it by appearing to levitate (it is up in the air, after all), creating a little garden magic while drawing attention to itself. Just as with containers placed on the ground, a suspended one also relies upon other design elements and nearby objects to round out the picture.

A dark-leaved begonia and its pot

the other colors, yet the dark begonia foliage echoes the arching leaves emerging from the right side of the pot on the ground, helping to unify the composition.

The uniform green of the almost perfect ball of succulents (*Aeonium castello-paivae*) comfortably fits within the space ⑲ at Ganna Walska Lotusland and adds interest

appear to float among the other items in this scene ⑱. The dark-colored, almost invisible, supports of the hanging container also add to the illusion; lighter-colored or more-complicated wires and other components would be more readily visible and could shatter the feeling of suspension. Note how the terra-cotta stands out among

to the archway without creating too much distraction. A more colorful and less regular shape—for example, a mixed basket of pansies with ivy trailing from it—would divert attention from the blue and white tiles and other details in this setting, disturbing the serenity of the scene.

Reminiscent of a school of jellyfish languidly pulsing above a group of sea anemones, several hanging containers of burro's tail sedum (*Sedum morganianum*) create an unforgettable tableau ⑳ also at Lotusland (see next page). Or are we looking at a group of ancient bearded mandarins discussing an important bureaucratic matter? Whatever image this picture conjures, the simple lines and staggered placement of the containers, as well as the inspired addition of the delicate conical coverings, reveal a masterful awareness of design and a subtle sense of humor.

A far cry from the airiness of sedum, this giant ball of coleus, dubbed the "tapestry ball" and designed by

Richard Hartlage, still creates a sense of suspension or floating . Using several kinds of coleus instead of just one lessens the impression of weight (compare this ball with the almost solid-colored one in the background). Also note that instead of several highly visible and distracting lines forming a blatant cone, the single (obviously very strong) chain presents just one, much less noticeable line, allowing the massive and colorful ball to dominate.

Sometimes a hanging container is

more than just an object used to suspend plants in midair; given the right container and an unexpected selection of plants, a composition may justifiably be characterized as art. These four pyramidal terra-cotta planters ㉒, again custom-designed by Hartlage for Washington Park Arbo-retum, barely contain a colorful explosion of orange impa-tiens, *Phormium* 'Jack Spratt', *Carex morrowii* 'Evergold', *Weigela florida* 'Rubidor', and *Heuchera* 'Palace Purple'. Why hang the usual when you can hang art?

THE IMPORTANCE OF
VANTAGE POINT

Although the pictures in this book present many container plantings from their most flattering side, the placement of a planting often allows a viewer to observe it from more than one vantage point or even in the round. A skillful designer creates a presentation attractive from a number of vantage points. Photos of individual plants also often eliminate much of the garden scene. Only by considering multiple photos of a particular garden—or by viewing the garden in person—can a more complete picture emerge of how a specific planting relates to its surroundings.

From the vantage point in image 23, the container planting stands out prominently against its architectural setting and the green backdrop. This angle allows the viewer to appreciate the attractive color combination, dramatic vertical movement, and visually engaging forms of the container planting, as well as to enjoy the interaction with the qualities of the wall, bench, and surface. It also permits a view of the nicely detailed container. The next picture 24 provides a totally different frame of reference, causing the planting to play a much less dominant role. The background and overall setting are now much more complicated, including a second (presumably matching) planting on the other side of the patio. It is not even readily apparent in this picture that the cannas (*Canna* 'Pretoria') grow in a container in combination with other plants. Other pictures taken from a third, or fourth, angle would certainly reveal even more details and visual interactions occurring in this setting.

If viewed close up, and at a quick glance, the pair of chartreuse-leaved

plants and their pots in the foreground here ㉕ illustrate a number of points relating to color, line, form, spacing, and relationship to the background and paved surface. However, this much wider view reveals that the pair is a segment of a circular arrangement that probably contains six or more members and serves as just a few of the many players in a much larger production. The characteristics of the pair of pots, although evident, must be perceived in the context of a much larger garden scene.

5: texture

The word "texture" may conjure up images of velvety leaves and spiny stems, but in this discussion it refers to the visual perception of fineness or coarseness and the many variations that occur along that spectrum. Picture a lace tablecloth, the intricate fronds of a maidenhair fern, or a narrow-bladed clump of grass: they are considered fine-textured because a great many individual, small, or narrowly linear parts make up the whole; thought of another way, their individual parts enclose a considerable amount of small spaces. Then, imagine a pile of large rocks, a rubber plant, or a large-leaved hosta: they belong at the coarse end of the continuum, with fewer large parts making up the whole or large areas of space—or none at all—contained between those parts. Like other design elements, texture interacts with the many qualities of a planting. For instance, plants with wavy leaf edges or lighter-colored or marked leaves generally appear finer than those with much simpler leaf edges and darker, solidly colored foliage. Whether subtle or obvious, texture contributes to the overall impression

your container planting conveys.

A fine-textured plant: The many individual, closely spaced leaflets ❶ give the Korean maidenhair fern (*Adiantum venustum*) a very delicate texture. Also note the very finely textured moss growing at its base.

And a very coarse one, with a twist: Big, broad leaves with a lot of space between them ❷ add up to a coarse texture. Note, how the thorns on the *Solanum quitoense* allay the coarseness, if only a little bit.

How does this ❸ golden variegated sage (*Salvia officinalis* 'Icterina') illustrate fine texture? Not only are the

leaves relatively small, numerous, and linear, containing many small spaces within the outline of the plant, but the yellow markings also help make the leaves look smaller than they are: at first glance, a viewer might see only the green parts and perceive the yellow markings as space.

Fine-textured plants seem to invite the viewer to touch and interact with them, making them good choices for easy-access settings. Their many parts and active appearance make them great specimen plants, especially when they can be seen close up. The greater the visual distance from a fine-textured plant, the more its individual parts and contained spaces appear to merge into a more solid, and therefore coarser, mass.

Placing this *Hakonechloa macra* 'Aureola' against the relatively uniform background of the gray tabletop and green lawn ④ allows the fine texture to stand out more prominently than if it were grouped with other plants or placed on a multicolored tablecloth. The plant's light color and its over-all sense of outward linear movement invite visitors to admire and interact with it.

Many distinct clusters of small, bright red flowers (*Pelargonium* 'Dorcas Brigham Lime') stand out vividly against the dark, solid mass of foliage ⑤, superimposing a fine textural feeling over a much coarser background. The brighter flowers create the illusion of space by shining like stars against the dark night sky. The ivy climbing the wall and the little variegated succulent at the base of the grouping demonstrate the textural influence of brighter coloration too: the creamy edges of the light green leaves cause them to look finer than would the foliage of a uniformly dark green selection. Also

look among the pots of succulents, where the many flowing lines of the almost grassy pencil cactus (*Rhipsalis* sp.) present a much finer appearance than the static, denser, coarser-looking rosettes of the other succulents.

Fine texture expresses itself in a variety of ways. Bringing two or more specimens together can create a visually pleasing picture, as long as the textures are different enough to produce contrasts that attract and hold the viewer's interest.

The plants in this grouping ⑥ exhibit fine texture for different reasons. Consider the many thin blades and light color of the grass (*Stipa tenuissima*), the small, pale-edged leaves of the coleus, and the intricately cut foliage and many small purple flowers of the *Solanum pyracanthum*. The variety of fine textures expressed by the three plants produces a pleasing study in the diversity available from the fine end of the textural spectrum. Contrast that to the monolithically (and perhaps monotonously) uniform presentation of three or more of the same plants.

Whereas fine textures give an impression of airiness, motion, and

delicacy, coarser ones suggest solidity, stability, and strength. A few large, dark, solid-colored, plain-edged leaves will not appear on the verge of floating away, so they can be used where a designer wants to make a strong statement.

Surrounded by mostly finer textures, a specimen of *Solanum quitoense* looks as stable as the Rock of Gibraltar ❼, making a suitable anchor at the end of a wall. A massive sculpture or garden ornament—think of a resting lion made of marble or a lead globe on a brick column—would make a similar statement, but lacking such inanimate pieces a clever garden designer can achieve a similar effect with a plant.

Although their cut edges imply fine texture, the big leaves of the artichoke relative *Cynara cardunculus* project a principally coarse feeling, especially when set within the context of many more-delicate examples ❽. So, too, do the nearly black leaves of the companion plant *Eupatorium sordidum*, with no readily perceivable size, cut-leaf edges, linear movement, or space between them.

TEXTURAL CONTRAST

Picture a finely cut parsley or dill leaf placed on a head of cabbage, or a white crocheted doily set on the arm of an overstuffed brown leather chair, and you will get the idea of textural contrast. Just as placing contrasting colors and forms next to each other can produce dramatic and attractive results, so too can juxtaposing finer and coarser textures, whether in the same container planting or among adjacent plantings and other garden elements.

It would be hard to find a more striking textural contrast than the one created by the agave (*Agave americana* 'Variegata') and the restio (*Chondropetalum tectorum* 'Cape Reed') at Heronswood Nursery ❾. The relatively few, large leaves of the agave seem to shout their strong coarseness, while the many slender stems of the restio almost whisper their fine texture. Of special interest is the reversal of one of the ways color helps create a perception of texture: the coarse plant bears the light-colored variegation (which helps tone down its coarseness), while the fine plant consists mostly of solid, rather dark green (which reduces the fine texture a

striped leaves. Viewed as a group, the three container plants present an eye-catching study in textural contrasts.

A range of textures makes for plenty of visual interest ⑪, in spite of these plants' small size. The delicate, fine-textured string of hearts (*Ceropegia linearis* subsp. *woodii*) and the even more aptly named string of beads (*Senecio rowleyanus*) contrast nicely with the slightly coarser, more linear spikes in the upper left and the still coarser, thick-leaved, tightly rosetted *Echeveria* spilling down the center of the terra-cotta container.

While employing contrast is a good way to highlight textural differences in a planting, using space and careful placement is another way to emphasize the textural qualities of a multiple-container planting. Arranging plants thoughtfully within each container and giving the containers some breathing room can bring out the best in all of the plants and make for a visually irresistible composition.

The plants in ⑫ and ⑬ (see next page) exhibit a range of textures and different ways to express those inherent textures (though more thought may have been given to one arrangement than the other).

bit). As a mental exercise, picture how the composition would look texturally if the agave were solid dark green and the restio a much lighter color, such as chartreuse, buff, or silvery gray.

Many little leaves and lavender flowers give the *Scaevola* 'Blue Fan' in the center ⑩ a very fine texture (especially evident in the drooping stem in front of the gray plinth), while the few big leaves of the *Solanum quitoense* to the left create a coarse look. The dracaena above the scaevola sits somewhere nearer the middle of the texture continuum, with its rather large but fairly numerous linear, color-

In the first picture, the linear leaves of the bright green grass in the center and the darker-leaved purple fountain grass (*Pennisetum setaceum* 'Purpureum') in the top right corner both produce a feeling of fine texture (in spite of their coloration occupying nearly opposite ends of the brightness spectrum). The little red flowers dotting the small-leaved, yellow-green *Pelargonium* 'Alpha') on the left also create a feeling of fineness. Although their leaves contain little space between them, both the *Solenostemon* (*Coleus*) 'Alabama Sunset' in the back and the *Houttuynia cordata* 'Chameleon' in the lower right-hand corner lie somewhere near the middle of the textural range, owing to their large numbers of leaves and the lighter markings on otherwise dark base colors. Coarse texture shows up in both the very dark-colored, few-leaved *Echeveria* and in the lighter but even fewer-leaved aloe (*Aloe ferox*) in the foreground. Although the plants present an appealing range of textures, it is not obvious where to look first or how to proceed among the abundance of textures, colors, and shapes.

In the second picture, finer textures appear among the small-leaved, silvery *Helichrysum* and the tiny-leaved, white-flowered *Angelonia* in the foreground container. Although respectively large, massive, and dark (all qualities that contribute to the perception of coarse texture), the *Phormium* 'Sundowner' and hydrangea (*Hydrangea anomala* subsp. *petiolaris*) nonetheless project rather fine textures. The phormium (in the rear pot) offers linear and variegated leaves, the hydrangea in the background bears many small leaves, and the tree yucca (*Yucca rostrata*) to the left displays a finely detailed surface on its trunk. Only the cream-edged *Plectranthus* in the foreground pot approaches textural coarseness, but even that feeling is diminished by the lighter variegation. So after studying this composition, is it surprising to realize that much of the textural quality falls nearer the fine range of the spectrum? Also note how grouping several smaller plants in one container and placing it among the larger, individually growing specimen plants, the hydrangea, and the bluestone surface create pleasant contrasts. This also encourages the viewer to spend some time admiring each component of the composition.

THE IMPACT OF DISTANCE ON TEXTURE

From a great enough distance even the most intricately detailed bleeding heart or threadleaf dill will fail to suggest fine texture. Distance creates the illusion of solidity as individual parts appear to merge together and the spaces between them are no longer evident. Keep this in mind as you create your compositions—your intentions may be quite different than observed reality.

Up close, the big, dark-leaved *Phormium* 'Pink Stripe' in ⑭ (see next page) would look quite coarse and bold in spite of its many linear leaves. The textural contrast with its container companion and its flowering and variegated neighbors reinforces this perception. However, this more distant view of this Heronswood Nursery (Washington State) planting attenuates that bold coarseness for several reasons: (1) the phormium becomes a smaller component of a much larger whole; (2) its linear quality echoes that of the smaller, indisputably fine-textured grasslike plants in the foreground; and (3) it no longer contrasts so sharply with its container companion or its neighbors. Instead of the phormium being a dominant (perhaps overbearing) object, it works as a focal point.

6: focal points

Just as a large jewel or colorful tie can become the center of attention in a clothing ensemble, so too can a carefully chosen container planting become the focus of all eyes in the garden. A container placed as a focal point draws you along a garden path or directs your vision to a particular spot, bringing attention to itself and often visually pulling together the area around it. Although sculptural and architectural features are often used as focal points in gardens large and small, a planted pot can be equally irresistible in the right spot in your garden.

So how do you take advantage of the design power of a focal point? Some gardens already have areas that by their very nature lend themselves to accommodating a focal point. Examples include a straight walkway or path, a lengthy double hedge or perennial border, or another similar long axis. Placing a focal point at the end of a relatively long view reinforces the visual depth of an axis, making it seem longer and perhaps grander than it already is. This has

been done by garden designers for centuries, including the famed André Le Nôtre at Versailles, Vita Sackville-West at Sissinghurst ❶ in southeast England, and Russell Page at the Donald M. Kendall Sculpture Garden (often called the PepsiCo Sculpture Garden) in Purchase, New York.

Focal points do not always occur at the end of a path or a view, though; they can also visually interrupt the uniformity of a wall or hedge, commanding attention.

Although other objects (specifically the lanterns and standard topi-

aries) break up the expanse of wall, there is no doubt that the giant bromeliad in the equally imposing urn is the first object you notice in this composition ❷. Your eyes may wander to the other objects, plants, and even to the brick paving, but your focus will inevitably return to the center of attention.

If you do not live in the midst of a formal garden, don't give up on the idea of using a focal point. In fact, small and simple gardens can benefit tremendously from the illusion of depth created by a focal point and

from its ability to tie various garden elements together. A container strategically placed within view from a patio, living-room window, or even your back steps will function as a focal point.

THE ROLE OF CONTRAST IN FOCAL POINTS

What follows is a brief foray into how to use the various elements of design to create strong focal points. Consider this first: once a container is planted and placed at the end of a view, within a group, or along a wall, what makes it work as a focal point? Color, line, form and mass, space, texture, and relative size can all simultaneously be in play at a focal point. Arguably, though, the one overarching factor that sets an element apart as the center of attention is contrast. And as we know contrast can be created using all of the elements of design.

Color

Picture a red marble in a handful of green ones, or a pink-sequined showgirl in the center of a line of tuxedo-clad male dancers, and you get the idea of how color provides contrast. Something unique in an otherwise uniform group cannot help but stand out. Similarly, a distinctively colored plant and pot automatically attract your eye and together become a focal point.

Note how the golden-foliaged *Pelargonium* 'Mrs. Cox' in ❸ contrasts strongly with the other plants and architectural features, becoming the focal point within many disparate elements. The pelargonium ties together what might otherwise be an arrangement lacking obvious unity. In ❹, however, no readily visible, contrasting element stands out, so the composition (from this angle, at least) lacks a focal point and coherence.

Pale-colored tulips (*Tulipa* 'Concerto') become the light-hearted center of attention ❺ when viewed alongside the dark-leaved cordylines and against the green of

the lawn behind them. Note how the purple tones of the violas, although not nearly as dark as the cordylines, play a supporting role to the much lighter shades of the tulips.

Even without the sun shining on them, the much brighter chartreuse leaves of the hosta ❻ jump from the darker green of the hedge. For an even stronger focal point, the hosta could be placed on a darker plinth.

Line

It is difficult to resist walking along or at least looking down a linear path. By their very nature, lines grab attention, especially if they exist in stark contrast to more elaborate, spacious shapes, such as circles or rectangles. Of course a line cannot by definition be a point, per se, but it can draw your eye to a focal point and so become part of the action.

Can't find the focal point? Follow the lines of the two gray steps toward the center **7** and then up the brownish trunk of the treelike succulent known as cabbage tree (*Cussonia paniculata*), and there sits the center of attention: the almost gushing mass of gray-green foliage. Try to picture the leaves as a mound without a trunk under

it. The foliage would not stand out nearly as well against the similarly colored blue-green plants above and below it. Here lines help make the point.

Form

Imagine a broad, uniform sweep of lawn or a long, uninterrupted wall (or even a plate of plain spaghetti). Then picture a piece of sculpture, such as a classical figure of the goddess Diana, placed in the lawn, or visualize a wall niche that houses a fountain or a trompe l'oeil painting. If you wish, conjure up a meatball in the middle of that plate of spaghetti. For whichever image you choose, it is the contrast in form that creates a focal point. It is easy to create container plantings that rely on contrast in shape to make a point: a round mass of coleus or other leafy plant set against a rectangular hedge will beg to be noticed.

Note how the distinctively spiky and almost melting shape of the agave (*Agave americana* 'Mediopicta') exists in stark contrast to the plain wall behind it **8**, diverting attention from the other objects. The lines in the paved floor, which clearly point in the direction of the agave, make the focal point even more irresistible and obvious.

Mass

Use mass to create contrast by placing a relatively uniform, simple, or easily recognizable body among a group of disparate elements, such as a bowl within a pile of silverware or a large, spreading-limbed tree against a background of fields, mountains, and sky. A large sculpture at the center of a complicated formal garden or an empty pot set within a colorful herbaceous border will do the same thing. Your

⑧

eye will gravitate to the denser, simpler, more massive part of the more complex whole.

A simple, uncluttered mass of *Echeveria secunda* var. *glauca* tumbling out of a pot ❾ becomes the focus of attention in an area composed of many small visual units (including the bricks and leaves on the wall). A feeling of languid repose, even decadence, further contributes to the planted container's dominance in the composition.

Space

A lot of space around an object helps draw attention to it, especially if the object is relatively simple and unclut-

tered: think of the visual power of a single sailboat on a large body of water, or the full moon in the sky, or one pea on an otherwise empty plate. The visual attraction of more-complex objects can be increased by setting them in an uncluttered space as well. In a readily perceivable way, the suggestion of loneliness increases the apparent attraction of an isolated container planting, creating a powerful focal point.

The dark color and dramatic shape of the black taro (*Colocasia esculenta* 'Black Runner') commands attention, but its solitary placement on the stone patio ❿ against the uncluttered wall leaves no doubt as to the designer's intent:

Look at this container! Try to picture the added spatial impact created by removing the plants at the base of the taro: the additional visible space between the plant and the pot would accentuate the feeling of solitude.

Texture

Far subtler than color, visual (not tactile) texture can create more subliminal yet still effective contrasts and focal points. Think of an intricate mosaic set within a plain, uniform wall or a feathery fern frond draped over a big, bold hosta leaf, and you will understand the power of texture in producing a focal point

Compared to its linear, cloudlike, and finer-textured neighbors, the rounded, almost lumpy, and coarser prickly pear (*Opuntia violacea*) is the attention-getter of this composition ⓫. This occurs in spite of its subtle blue-green coloration and finely dotted pattern on the pads. The prickly pear's relatively small size fails to diminish its ability to serve as the focal point.

Relative Size

A nine-hundred-pound gorilla will always command attention. So too will a large object set among any number of smaller ones: imagine a grapefruit alongside a couple of grapes or an oak towering over a grassy field. Place a big pot of cannas in a bed of dwarf marigolds, and your eye will be immediately drawn to the big boy.

A gigantic bromeliad (sp. *Vriesea*) dominates by sheer virtue of its size ⓬. Only after digesting the impact of such a big plant does the viewer notice the attractive shape and pleasing contrast provided by the square-sided pot. Compared to the bromeliad, the other plants look like munchkins.

TOO MUCH OF A GOOD THING?

It has been said "If one is good, then two must be better." This adage sometimes works with focal points and some-

times does not. When two nearly identical objects are placed next to each other, they can easily cancel each other out, producing unnecessary duplication instead of a powerful, unified effect. The eye is drawn to the existence of two objects, which can lead to visual confusion and dilution. Observers might ask themselves, "Why are there two objects here? Is there a path or other feature between the two objects? Is there another set of two somewhere else in the garden that I should look for?" As a general rule, avoid confusion by placing only one object at a focal point.

The concept that two is not always better than one is illustrated by this pair of *Cordyline australis* 'Albertii' ⑬ . Cover the left-hand cordyline to see how dramatically the remaining one stands out from the rest of the scene. A picture taken more to the left in this garden, looking directly at the two cordylines, would probably reveal the intended use of the two plants as a stunning pair of objects flanking the top of a flight of stone stairs or marking the entryway to a garden space beyond. From the angle of this picture, however, the pair does not function as an effective focal point.

That said, it is possible to effectively use two or three—or, if you are very skilled, many—items in one spot as a focal point. When using a pair, be sure to make one of objects perceptibly but not dramatically different than the other, and when using a group, be sure that one item appears noticeably different than the others, which should all be quite uniform.

Chiefly because of their identical coloration, these two planters ⑭ work together to produce a single focal point. Extra interest comes from the dissimilar yet visually

balanced sizes, shapes, and contents of the planters. The differences are not great enough, though, to distract from the power of the focal point.

FIGHTING FOR ATTENTION

A focal point should be just that—a point—or at least a relatively contained area that draws attention to itself by displaying a readily perceived characteristic, such as a dramatic color or intriguing shape. Two nonidentical but similar objects may function as a focal point, but there should not be several noticeable differences among the objects. It is especially important to avoid combining two or more dissimilar colors, or you may have a visual war on your hands.

Where is the focal point here **15**? Is it the bright yellow violas or perhaps the vibrant orange pansies? The two pots of more subtly colored pansies vie for attention as well, although not as obviously. While this is certainly a very colorful collection of pansies and violas, this grouping does not serve as a cohesive focal point.

THE POWER OF NOVELTY

Lest you come to think that a focal point always sits regally at the end of a view, commands attention in the center of a given area, or nestles snugly into a niche, remember that rules and conventions can always be broken, particularly by an inspired designer. Placing an object before the end of a vista or in the foreground of a view can create a memorable focal point.

Although the rustic pergola-topped bench at the end of this view **16** could nicely serve by itself as a conventional focal point, it plays a subservient role to the single pot of dwarf boxwood (*Buxus microphylla* var. *japonica* 'Morris Midget') placed in the middle of the brick walk. The actual

focal point occurs not at the end of the view but—dramatically—between the viewer and the end of the view. Note the very simple combination of the rather plain plant and pot; a flashier plant and/or more elaborate container would amount to overkill.

The foreground, and not the more usual background, can offer the setting for a focal point **17**. A pot of *Ajania pacifica* placed on an ivy-covered pillar in the foreground of

this setting commands as much attention as would a red-flowered tree or rushing waterfall at the far end of the view.

IS THIS A FOCAL POINT?

Remember that gardens and landscapes are not photographs: they are three-dimensional spaces through which we move and, in so doing, experience an ever-changing series of images and emotional reactions. What may not look like a focal point from one angle may well shout out as one from another. Because of their portability, container plantings make very adaptable focal points. If a container does not meet your expectations in a specific spot, it can be moved a foot or two or across the garden to find its perfect placement.

From the angle shown here ⓲, you might not be drawn to the large pot of orange spikes (bromeliad *Aechmea* sp.) above arching green leaves: other elements, such as the two columns or the bright orange cannas, vie for your attention. Yet seen from the other side ⓳ (see next page), the large pot—minus the two columns and other distractions—

exists without question as the center of attention. Moving yourself around a garden, or moving container plantings to different sites, provides a variety of interactive experiences with focal points and other design elements.

EMPTY CONTAINERS

Must a container be planted for it to attract attention and function as a focal point? The answer is no. Just as a piece

of sculpture or specimen plant may draw your eye, so too can an empty container, sometimes more effectively than if it were planted. (The next chapter discusses the appeal of emptiness more fully.)

By virtue of its placement as well as its black-hole emptiness, the unplanted spherical container serves as the unquestioned center of attention in this setting **20**. Had it been planted and placed more upright, it would exist as just another element in a less memorably unified garden.

⑳

7: the appeal of emptiness

Let's think outside the box for a little while to consider the use and appeal of some unplanted garden pieces. Although none of the elements highlighted in this chapter hold plants, all of the examples can be viewed in the same design terms as those for planted pots.

Without the distraction presented by an obvious plant cargo, an empty container gives the observer a chance to interact with it as he or she might with a piece of sculpture or similar art object. In so doing, the piece can elicit a range of feelings or even emotions that a bust, ruined column, or modern metal sculpture might also conjure. Reacting to an object in a garden setting is not limited to monumental, massive pieces; even a small but visually interesting and thoughtfully placed item will engage a perceptive observer. In a garden the opportunities for placement are limited only by the creativity of the designer. Group your unplanted garden piece or empty container with plants, other containers, and garden features to bring out the best in every component of a garden composition or area.

Almost Euclidean in their simple geometry, two spherical pieces  make as strong a statement—maybe even more potent—than a pot of bright flowers or an attractively shaped foliage plant. The pieces, made by Little and Lewis for Heronswood Nursery, are essentially the same color as a common terra-cotta pot, but subtle differences in shading set them apart: The smaller pot in front is a bit warmer-toned and more uniformly colored than the larger one, which features contrasting darker and lighter areas. The emptiness of the front piece allows it to present a jagged-edged, almost black contrast to the terra-cotta shades. Likewise, the lines of the two pots produce an engaging contrast between their soft, rounded silhouettes and the hard, ragged edges around the openings, most dramatically shown in the front container but subtly echoed in the back one. Their rounded, massive shape immediately invokes a feeling of strength and stability (or maybe they look soft and voluptuous to you?), and the lack of space between the two pieces (at least from this angle) suggests cohesion and unity. A more active expression of space takes place in the black hole of the front pot. A planted pot does not show the space contained within it, but an empty pot certainly can. Both pieces have a rather coarse surface, making their placement next to the very fine-textured restio all the more brilliant. Additionally, the dark green foliage creates a pleasing color contrast, and the brownish stems almost subliminally pick up on the terra-cotta of the pots. The plant's numerous lines and many little spaces among its branches reinforce the textural contrast with the much simpler spherical pieces.

Does this composition suggest simplicity, repose, and union, or does it give a feeling of strength and perhaps even conflict? And which sort of creature, modern or ancient, hatched out of those "eggs"?

This massive urn ❷ does not need to hold any plants to attract and hold a viewer's interest. Thoughtful placement makes for a visually interesting composition. Its rich bronze hue stands out among the surrounding colors, including the different shades of green in the three arching *Phormium tenax* and the color of the house behind.

On the other hand, the bronzy brown blends nicely with the brick of the patio and the wall. With its smooth surface and uniform silhouette, the container does not suggest any texture. Its very simple silhouette is broken only slightly by the small opening at the top. The massive form gives no impression of space (save for the implication of hollowness made by the opening), but it dominates the space around it. The simple line and massive, spaceless form stand in stark contrast to the much more complicated and less imposing plants and patio. No doubt the contrast would exist from almost any angle.

So is the piece in the composition the odd man out, or more like big man on campus or ruler of the roost? Does it seem alone and standoffish, or is it the center of attention? Perhaps you perceive something quite different.

The urn's dark, muddy coloration ③ might register as unattractive to some, but the complicated silhouette and ornamentation present plenty of linear detail, producing a more intricate yet still substantial form. No suggestion of space is created, save for

that below the bowl, and its texture must be considered coarse here. So what makes this piece worthy of consideration, even admiration? Personal preferences aside, the sharp contrasts generated between the urn and its physical context do attract attention. Compare the dead color of the urn with the much warmer earthy splotches on the plinth and the neatly matching wall behind it. Then consider the contrast generated with the bright green of the moss overtaking the bricks. The curved fluting and swagging on the urn oppose the sharply angled lines of the plinth and bricks but subtly harmonize with the bowed seat and wall. The urn's much more complex form jumps out at the viewer, and although it projects little of its own space, it dominates the space around it. Coarse texture abounds in this picture, with no strong contrast apparent, although the splotches on the plinth and the wall and the bricks below, suggest a slightly finer texture.

Does this composition suggest anything other than a cold, foreboding feeling, similar to what one might experience in an ancient cemetery? Or

perhaps it evokes images of an eighteenth-century English lord surveying his estate, or maybe a Roman senator standing in the Forum? Do you even focus your attention on the urn after a while? Perhaps you instead begin to concentrate on the mental pictures the splotches conjure up. In any case, you must admit that this simple arrangement—totally devoid of contained plants—offers much to view and consider.

A dark urn covered with moss rises out of an uninterrupted expanse of green at Heronswood ④. Its silhouette brings together several curved

lines and a circle at the opening, creating a very dense, rather substantial form. Like other similar containers, the urn incorporates very little noticeable space except for the tiny bit within the handle; what space it does contain within its exterior appears barely perceptible in the darkness. Shades of gray-black and the delicate green growth punctuate an otherwise texture-free surface. Once again, the urn's placement rescues the container from anonymity. The sea of bright green, its expanse broken only by even brighter shadows, sets off the pot, as do the varied lines and forms of the

flora around the pool. A large, empty space above the pool draws attention to both the pot and the plants. The fine-textured plants that appear to be entering the mouth of the container contrast with the nearly featureless pot and pool.

Does this pot suggest to you a creature emerging from the water to feed? Or do you get the feeling that you have stumbled onto the ruins of an ancient civilization suddenly destroyed by some cataclysmic event? Whatever the perception, the container—and its moody setting—evokes an image or feeling that no planted pot in this place could.

Three pots sit at an entrance designed by Steve Martino, with only an ocotillo (*Fouquieria splendens*) keeping them company ❺. So what is of interest here? The understated pots may not clamor for attention, but the coloration of each, whether uniformly dark or minimally marked with other colors, possesses a richness that combines intriguingly with the others. Their simple lines and unadorned forms make equally quiet but interesting statements. They express space only in terms of the air

that surrounds them, and they do not bring to mind the concept of "texture." Once again, thoughtful placement makes this group interesting. The pale gray concrete provides a foil that heightens the colors of the pots, while the sunlight on the concrete relieves the monotony of the pallid gray. The ocotillo's form, composed of a mass of nearly straight lines (serendipitously duplicated on the back wall by the shadows, which at first glance look like another plant emerging from the black container) powerfully contrasts with the curvaceous pots and is subtly echoed on the edges of the steps and the walls. All of the objects

exist within a simple, uncluttered, noncompetitive space. The large area of fine texture that is created by the spaces contained among the ocotillo's branches and their shadows stands in dramatic contrast to the almost featureless pots.

Does this simplicity register positively with you, or do you find it boring? Is it welcoming or off-putting? Although devoid of bright flower colors and or a variety of leaf textures, a composition like this one can still command a great deal of attention and invite closer inspection.

Sometimes you can have a little bit of fun while offering viewers what

initially seems like a very simple, understated composition. An elegant vessel ⑥ (see previous page) mixes soft, earthy colors within a simple silhouette that defines a curvaceous, solid form. Little space is evident, and no texture immediately stands out. Simple but pleasing, don't you think? A closer look reveals much more than first meets the eye. The vessel actually exhibits many shades of brown and yellow, and even some blue, applied in a highly detailed pattern on the surface as well as on the rim and handle. The rounded sides and circular top and handle echo each other, and the

very solid form of the pot's body provides a backdrop for the delicately textured patterns of the rim and handle. The handle also surrounds a little bit of space. Best of all—and here is where the fun comes in—instead of existing as an empty but nonetheless attractive container in the garden, it is filled to the top with water, providing a mirrored surface to reflect the luxuriant, rich green ivy framing the pot. It's the miragelike, "made you look" quality of the water that takes this "empty" container to a new and very engaging level.

Could you resist the temptation to float something on

the surface of the water? A flower or leaf or candle would add another element of interest to the composition, but it would also interfere with, or maybe even eliminate, the surprising mirror illusion.

While subtlety is soothing and oh-so-very tasteful, sometimes even the most understated of gardeners appreciates an in-your-face yet highly sophisticated expression of glee. While an exuberantly colorful and dynamic pot of plants can achieve that result, so too can an empty container.

Every design element comes vigorously into play in this composition ❼, and the result is undeniably exciting. A bright blue wash spices up a terra-cotta urn composed of very simple lines (two curved ones topped by a straight one), which define a massive form that encloses no visible space. The blue suggests a fine texture for what would otherwise be a featureless surface. Although this container would make a statement no matter where it was placed, its position in this garden allows it to express its qualities more readily. The blue bench and columns accentuate the blue wash on the pot, as do the bright

green leaves of the *Darmera peltata* in the foreground and yellow-toned plants on the right and in the background. While the columns appear straight-sided, our mind's eye wants to fill in the details of their rounded forms, complementing the sides of the pot. The rectilinear bench echoes the straight line of the top of the pot, too. Rounded- and linear-leaved plants continue the interplay of line and form. As with most empty containers, the space around this pot sets it off, and the many different plant textures contrast attractively with the minimally textured container.

Would you ever include brightly colored pots, benches, and columns in your garden? If you wanted to make a strong statement using a certain color but could not grow suitably hued plants, using colorful pots and maybe other objects—might produce your desired result.

Don't hide an attractive pot in your shed or storage room just because you don't have the right plant for it. Empty pots or other unplanted garden objects can make as much of a statement—perhaps even more—as a planted pot.

Sleight of hand and twist of fate: who would expect to see a leaf appearing to float in midair inside a piece like this ❽? Of course the leaf is floating on water, but the dark interior and lack of any reflection creates the illusion of weightlessness. This is the same piece shown from a distance in an earlier photo (page 94). Not only does the container play the role of focal point when viewed at a distance, but it becomes a conversation point up close. Who knows which little treasure might have been featured here before or after this picture was taken? Simplicity and unexpected drama often make a masterpiece.

part ii:
bringing it all together

8: designs that work

How do you know when a container planting works? Perhaps simply looking at the planting gives you a positive, satisfied feeling: "It looks nice and makes me feel good taking care of it, so I like it." Or maybe you use it as a test laboratory, observing it to see how the plants grow and relate to each other, the container(s), and the surroundings: "It grows and therefore teaches me, so I like it." Perhaps, like me, you enjoy observing and analyzing your own gardening as well as others', asking yourself how a planting comes together (or not) from both design and emotive standpoints: "The colors and lines make this grouping look like lava oozing down a hillside, so I like it." Whatever your approach, what follows are several examples of container plantings and my evaluations of their design elements. I will let you decide if the compositions work for you visually and perhaps on a deeper emotional level.

At first glance this diagonal grouping ❶ may not immediately grab a viewer's attention; the colors don't necessarily jump out. While a few

spots of color pop out from behind the diagonal row of pots, they do not add to the cohesion of the overall scene but instead create distraction. However, the various green shades in the row of potted plants help tie the grouping together visually. From this angle, the strong diagonal line running from lower right to upper left makes a much stronger statement than many expressions of color would. The circular lines in the hardscaping add another aspect of movement as well. Line also plays an important part in the individual linear components and the rounded silhouettes of the cordyline (*Cordyline australis* 'Albertii') and the golden bamboo grass (*Hakonechloa macra* 'Aureola') in the front. These, in particular, stand out among the indistinct lines and shapes of the plants in the middle and subtly pick up on the very formal mounded gumdrop topiary in the back. Space feels abundant here: within the outline of the spiky cordyline, between the three groups of pots, and all around the diagonal row of pots (more detectable along the more visible front side). Fine texture dominates the group, but the dense standard topiary in the back

and nearby containers add some coarseness to the mix. The grouping does not function as a focal point: it is too long and complex. The pots of orange flowers and the rustic arbor seat, as well as the pink flowers, grab attention in this setting.

Although there is much to say about this diagonal container planting, the brick patio could be considered the most distinct attribute of this garden setting. It is big and spacious, simple and elegant, and provides the setting for the containers that ornament it and the beds that surround it. Place your hand over the foreground plants and the standard topiary in the back to see how the patio could make its presence felt even more.

Two container plantings at the corner of a house ❷ stand out from their surroundings, though not obtrusively; the understated shades of mostly dark green contrast gently with the light brown of the pots. Those colors in turn exist quietly different from the paint on the house shingles. No bright colors or brilliant contrasts here! The pots exhibit strong lines, both in their silhouettes and on their surfaces, which both

the fern on the left and the peace lily (*Spathiphyllum*) on the right pick up and carry upward and outward. The vine (pothos) tumbling out of the pot on the right diverts the eye and lessens the upward movement of the lily. Without the downward movement of the pothos, the lily would appear even more energetic. Although the plant shapes contain enough visual interest to attract the eye, the forms of the pots (drawing upon a strong presence of line) hold the viewer's attention longest. The only suggestion of space occurs at the tops of the two principal plants, especially where the house number shows through. No space exists between the plants, and little space seems to surround them because so many other objects appear in the background (another camera angle might reveal a broad space in front of the pots). The fine "feathers" of the fern sit on the other end of the textural spectrum from the coarse "paddles" of the peace lily and the dense foliage of the pothos.

No design element in this grouping calls out for attention. Both pots, by virtue of their closeness to each other and their harmony of design

elements, draw the eye away from the many other objects in this setting and provide a focal point. The simple combination of the two pots and their plants attracts the viewer's eye and helps unify the complicated, detailed background.

This composition ❸ goes for the gusto. Color has been used in large, bold strokes against a rather uniformly dark green canvas. Though not readily obvious, the three principal colors of the red-violet *Allium* 'Globemaster', the blue-green in the centers of the agave leaves, and the muted red-orange of the containers compose a triadic harmony. The straight lines

of the allium stems echo the edges of the pots and the more curvaceous yet still linear agave leaves. The circular outlines of the allium flower heads subtly resemble the rounded outlines of the agaves. Spheres (the alliums) and cubes (the pots) take the two-dimensional lines into the third dimension of form, with the agaves borrowing qualities from both solids and providing a transition from one group of purer shapes (spheres) to the other (cubes). Space abounds among the allium flower heads and between the agave leaves, and the spacing of the agaves indicates that some distance separates the pots as well.

Even though the camera is quite near to the grouping, and the alliums grow closely with the background plants, the abundant visual space prevents this composition from feeling claustrophobic. Scores of little blossoms lighten the texture of the dense allium flower heads, while the tiny teeth on the agave leaves soften the coarseness of their edges. From this vantage point, the composition does not function as a focal point—there are far too many individual components—but it might become a focal point if viewed from a greater distance, as the separate purple spheres and pots of agave merge into more unified masses.

Placing three nearly identical pots of agave next to a planting of allium creates a simple yet powerful garden composition. Try to imagine what this picture would look like if the allium flowers were pale yellow or the agaves were replaced with pots of trailing ivy. What if the pots were spherical, or the alliums grew in a solid mass, or the pots contained delicate maidenhair ferns? Then try to envision the impact of combining other flowers with the alliums and grouping other plants in different containers with the potted agaves. None of the three principal players are complex, yet bringing them—and only them—together in this way allows their widely contrasting qualities to combine, creating a pleasing whole.

It is always fun to put a twist on a conventionally held notion, as this combination ❹ boldly does. Complementary yellow and purple, which I learned as a kid were Easter colors—especially when light and springlike in feeling—create even more visual energy when placed within a dark-toned setting. The purple violas and yellow daffodils (*Narcissus* 'Hawera') seem to glow against the mass of *Cordyline australis*. The jagged silhouettes of the cordylines and the circles suggested by the pot rims add to the visual energy, as does the contrast between the open, spiky shapes behind the dense, rounded forms in the front (including the pots). Although the containers are placed close together, the openness of the cordylines adds a feeling of space, as does the pots' placement near the lawn and stone edging. Textures range from very fine (the daffodils), to between fine and coarse (the violas), to much coarser (the cordylines), to nonexistent (the pots), making a stimulating interplay. The bright yellow flowers probably function as a focal point from ten or more feet back. At first glance, the only discordant note in this composition arises from the rawness of the terra-cotta pot containing the violas. However, a closer look reveals a second terra-cotta pot of violas and another similar one holding the middle cordyline, so the repetition helps lessen the discord.

Great designers may begin a project by considering commonly and predictably used objects and principles, but they often move beyond the familiar and expected to make a new and distinctive statement. Combining spring-blooming plants in strong colors with summery-looking cordylines and other plants of an unabashedly nonspring-like color produces an unexpected and visually arresting garden scene.

If you have ever doubted the power that a couple of simply planted pots can hold in a garden spot, perhaps this composition ❺ will convince you. Not only does the sunny grouping of yellow and white in the Juno irises (*Iris bucharica*) irresistibly draw the eye, but the placement against the neutral, almost somber stone steps makes the combination seem to leap forward. The bright green leaves stand out against the steps and provide a clean, cheerful foil for the flowers (the green of the irises appears more "alive" than the other foliage colors). Even the pots, although not brightly colored, provide a pleasant contrast for their cargo and interact nicely with the steps. Arching lines of foliage very subtly mirror the curving pot sides; like their coloration, the softer, more animated, curved lines of the irises provide

a noticeable contrast to the stronger, less active parallel lines of the steps. Although the form of the irises may not be as striking as, say, a weeping tree or a conical conifer, the simplicity of the containers emphasizes the flowers' shape more so than would complicated (visually distracting) pots. Little space appears within the mass of irises but plenty of it surrounds them, so much so that space becomes an unusually important component in this design. Placing the pots

along the lengthy flight of steps and shooting the picture at this angle also contributes to the feeling of space; the pots almost hang in the air. Lying in the middle of the textural spectrum between the coarse stone steps and the much finer shrubs alongside, the irises mediate between—perhaps even unify—the other objects. The design elements of the two pots of irises combine to create an indisputable focal point, don't you think? To see how the same garden space appears with other container-grown plants of a very different color, see the picture of colchicums on page 186.

Creating a distinctive and beautiful garden scene does not require a lot of plants, pots, or space. Placing a few—or sometimes just one—simply planted and constructed container in a complementary setting can produce more visual pleasure and ambiance than a dozen less carefully chosen pots set within a competing framework. Less is sometimes more.

This scene ❻ could be a poster child for container gardening. Bright red lily-flowered tulips ('Marjolein') and yellow-edged cordylines (*Cordyline australis* 'Albertii') catch fire in front of a dark, undifferentiated background. Notice the gray-leaved dusty miller (*Centaurea gymnocarpa*) on the right: not only does its soft hue provide a foil for the scene's brighter colors, but the decidedly blue cast of the leaves becomes the third member of a primary triadic harmony. Also, the green tulip foliage combines with the plants in the foreground to anchor the bright colors and frame the rim of the terra-cotta pot. (How would this grouping look if we could see more of the pot?) Two sets of powerful straight lines—parallel in the tulip stems and arising from a central point in the cordyline—create a highly kinetic feeling, while the much softer and less formally arranged lines of the grass in the foreground seem to loll peacefully. The tulip leaves suggest a feeling of uncontrolled or highly exuberant movement. All of the active lines fall along a vigorously moving diagonal bounded by the curved silhouettes of the plants on either side. Interacting with the many lines are the prominent rounded shapes of the cordyline, the dusty miller, and the *Hebe sutherlandii*, as well as the (initially) less obvious rectangular groups of the tulip flowers and their stems. Not much space exists here, except for the dark areas above the cordyline; wider spacing would almost certainly break the continuity of the energetic diagonal line and greatly diminish the appeal of this combination. The finer textures of the dusty miller, the hairlike *Stipa tenuissima,* and the hebe contrast strongly with the much coarser tulips and cordyline, while the nearly featureless backdrop sets everything off. From this distance the cordyline and tulips vie for the role of focal point but from a greater distance, the two probably join forces visually and produce one irresistible bull's eye.

So why is this combination such an excellent example of container gardening at its best? In addition to possessing all of the design merits discussed, this arrangement does not take up much room and so could be recreated or emulated in a small garden as well as in a much larger one. Both pots can also be relocated if desired (a useful feature of most containers). In this case the tulips can be removed when they have faded and can be replaced by a similar or disparate pot of something else. If the spirit moves, the cordyline or any other potted plant could be moved as well. Any large hedge, screen, or wall can provide the backdrop for a grouping like this one, as would a large expanse of lawn. The gardener might buy a pot or two of tulips or perhaps force them at home. The cordyline could be purchased annually (deep pockets and local source willing), or it could be a treasured plant protected inside every winter.

A well-thought-out composition like this one takes gardening to a higher level. Beyond offering colors and lines and shapes and other qualities for enjoyment, a carefully composed garden scene can conjure up images in a viewer's imagination. Perhaps it reminds you of a long-ago Fourth of July fireworks display or, more abstractly, of a woodland stream cascading madly between boulders on a mountainside. What you might see in a garden scene depends, of course, on your own imagination and experiences.

9: other sensory elements

Previous chapters have illustrated the elements of color, line, form, space, and visual texture and also have explored creating focal points and using unplanted pots. Other sensory elements—namely motion, sound, fragrance, taste, and tactile qualities—can't really be captured photographically, but they deserve at least a brief mention. Such sensory elements can add greatly to or significantly diminish the overall ambiance of a garden.

MOTION

Leaves and flowers flutter in the breeze. Tall grasses sway in the wind. Birds dash and hop between the earth and sky. Butterflies move languidly or resolutely zoom from one bloom to the next. Water erupts in lively jets or soothingly trickles from a fountain. The rods and cones of our retinas, stimulated by photons, send messages to our brains, translating these actions into perceptions of motion. And while the visible, linear qualities of plants, pots, and structures can suggest movement, only live, real-time motion can truly animate a garden. Movement in the garden can be savored as an ever-present dance.

Container gardeners can accentuate motion by placing pots of grasses and cordylines in breezy spots, allowing morning glories and black-eyed Susan vines to sway from hanging baskets, and by enticing butterflies to visit heliotropes and lantanas in sunny spots. Let your garden move, and it will in turn move you.

SOUND

Leaves rustle. Bamboo clashes. Birds sing. Bees hum. Water gurgles. Music plays. Arising from motion—of patterns of air molecules bumping around in our inner ears that in turn send nerve impulses to our brains—sound brings another dimension of the physical world to life. As fleeting as motion, sound creates feelings of mystery (where did that sound come from?), pleasure (a mockingbird sing-

1 The medium-height, bright orange *Dahlia* 'David Howard' brings some elevated color and bobbing motion to a planting.

2 Leafy palm fronds and fatsia make rustling sounds as a breeze moves through them.

ing to the morning), and repose (the gentle hum of cicadas in summer). It also conjures deeper, perhaps indefinable, memories and sensations of days gone by. Let your container gardens rustle and clash, sing and hum, gurgle and play. Some day in the future a sound may take you back to a treasured garden memory.

FRAGRANCE

Roses. Jasmines. Heliotropes. Gardenias. Daffodils. Pizza. Chocolate-chip cookies. Science tells us that we perceive fragrance when airborne molecules stimulate olfactory receptors deep within our noses, which then generate nerve impulses that tell our brains of the nearness of a bouquet, a bonfire, or a bad apple. Countless volumes of prose and poetry sing the praises of fragrant flowers and the spells they cast, but gardeners know the equally powerful appeal of scented leaves—such as rosemary, mint, and lemon verbena— and fragrant fruits, roots, and bark.

Like sounds, fragrances may come and go almost before we realize their presence, or they can hang in the air seemingly forever. Known scientifi-

cally as a limbic sensation, smell is the sense most strongly associated with memory, capable of mentally transporting us to a bygone place and time. To this day, the rich, sweet fragrance of gardenias immediately reminds me, almost tangibly, of both my grandmothers.

You can set the stage for your own personal limbic experiences—or warm fuzzies; call them what you will—by tending a rose garden, forcing pots of hyacinths, trimming a myrtle into a standard topiary, allowing moonflowers to climb over a bamboo teepee in a whiskey barrel, or locating an herb garden near your kitchen window. Just be sure to take time to smell the roses or the (insert your favorite here).

TASTE

Sweet. Sour. Salty. Bitter. *Umami* (the fifth quality Japanese researchers have proposed to cover "savory"). Your taste buds pick up molecules and send messages over that busy nerve highway to the brain. Your brain then does the job of sorting out the various percentages of basic tastes into specific sensations of mint or rosemary, brussel sprouts or pan-seared scallops, or any other of an enormous catalog of taste experiences.

While this book does not explore the triumphs and tribulations of growing fruits and vegetables and other edibles in your garden, don't deny yourself the pleasure of tasting a cherry tomato right off the container-grown vine or using fresh thyme and basil from a little pot on the porch stoop. Some tasty plants smell good too, reminding us that our senses of taste and smell work together to produce pleasant or not-so-pleasant sensations. By growing a few edible

plants among your garden containers, not only will you add to your kitchen pots, you will add another invisible dimension to your overall garden atmosphere.

TOUCH AND TACTILE QUALITIES

Mmmm. Ouch! Ooooooooooh. Ugh! Aaaaah. Various bundles of nerves in our skin pick up our interactions

with the surface qualities of objects in our world and send unmistakable messages of pleasure or pain, silky smoothness or alligator roughness, to our brains. Like sound and fragrance, tactile sensations can invite us to come closer or can steer us away. Who can deny the soft, gentle appeal of a lamb's fluffy coat (that of an actual animal or the leaves of lamb's ears) or the shock of a sudden sting from a thistle or sharp-spined cactus? Like sound and fragrance, tactile sensations often evoke strong, very personal emotions and memories. While not as actively perceived and traditionally celebrated as motion, sound, and fragrance, touch has its place in the garden. Pause to stroke a thread-leaved sedge, sticky petunia, or rough lantana. In the process you might release a fragrance, doubling your sensory experience.

③ Cut-leaf basil provides interesting texture in a container, as well as fragrance and taste.

④ *Furcraea foetida* 'Mediopicta' appears to explode from its pot—and its leaf tips won't draw blood in a close encounter!

10: expert container techniques

Generally speaking, it is not as easy living life in a pot as it is in the ground. Unlike a plant in the open garden, a plant in a container cannot stretch out its roots to search for water and nutrients. The sides of the pot might as well be a two-foot-thick steel door for most plants, and the drainage hole serves as a source of respite only for those plants whose roots can grow out into underlying soil. Even then, plenty of container gardens rest on decks and stone patios or hang in the air, where penetrating into underlying soil is not an option.

The very essence of a container garden elevates even the greenest of gardeners to the Provider of Necessary Things. While rain may fall from the sky (but not always when needed or in sufficient amounts), a good balanced fertilizer doesn't. And while the sun certainly shines (or doesn't) regardless of a gardener's desires, we are the ones who must site a container garden in the appropriate spot. Don't attempt to grow a shade-loving fern on a sunny south-facing deck or a cactus in a dark north-facing corner of a patio. You wouldn't place your vegetable patch in dark shade or try to grow African violets outside in Minnesota in January, would you? By the same token, don't try to grow a fern with a cactus or a marigold and a pansy together in the same pot: one of the two, and maybe both, will suffer from the effects of overabundance or deprivation. Though adaptable, a container planting still must abide by certain laws of nature. So while many plants can manage for themselves quite nicely in the open garden, container plants must be managed more attentively.

The extra attention required by this type of gardening is balanced by its flexibility. You love bougainvillea but don't live anywhere near the tropics? No problem! Grow it outside in a pot during the warm, sunny months and remember to provide winter protection for it. Do this for any treasured plant that wouldn't stand a snowball's chance in a hot place if left outside to fend for itself year round. Do your pink begonias and orange coleus look terrible together after a few weeks in the pot? Try combining the begonias with lavender angelonia in one pot and the coleus with 'Dark Opal' basil in another before the season progresses too far. Does your spectacular variegated agave look dumpy in a chipped, salt-stained pot? Give it a handmade gray-toned pot or a shiny dark blue one and then admire both plant and pot as an art object. Maybe you are going to host a big party in July but will be away from home during the month of August. If so, put together some containers in spring and grow them into beautiful, portable decorations for the party and then give them away, hire a plant sitter for them, or even discard them before you leave for vacation. If gardening provides an outlet for your creativity and experimentation, container gardening can allow you to express yourself to the fullest.

No matter how creative you are with your plant combinations and pot selections, and placement, your plants will not thrive—much less survive—if they do not receive the care they need. While not attempting to be exhaustive, the following pages offer essential information and

① An established clump of *Xanthosoma* 'Lime Zinger' provides an attractive contrast for the blue pot that awaits it.

some specialized tips that will help neophytes, veterans, and everyone in between become better container gardeners. Remember, whether they grow in the ground or in a pot, when you give your plants the sustenance and conditions they need to thrive, both you and the plants stand a good shot at happiness.

THE FIRM FOUNDATION: BASIC SOIL COMPOSITION AND WATER MOVEMENT

Although it may look like a solid mass, any good potting mix (or "dirt," or "soil," or "medium," or whatever you choose to call it) contains a surprising amount of air. Roots require air to perform their functions, which include water uptake and making more roots, and without enough air they decline and die. The same spaces that contain air sometimes also hold water, which is just as necessary. But air and water don't just sit there; they move through a potting mix as water enters, drains out, evaporates, or is taken up by plants. Some plants thrive in very open, airy mixes that let water move rapidly through them, while others grow very well in denser, more compacted mixes that retain water much longer.

Water does not drain from a pot exactly like it does in the open ground. In the garden, water goes downward, or percolates, throughout a relatively indefinite mass of soil. In a pot, water likewise moves down but exits (as a liquid) only through the drainage hole (if present and functional). Slow or impeded drainage may be a container-grown aquatic plant's dream, but it is a nightmare for plants that need more air around their roots. Three factors contribute to good drainage in a pot:

Plenty of pore space in the potting mix. Mixes containing a large percentage of bark, coir (composted coconut fiber), perlite, pumice, or vermiculite (the last three being expanded mineral products) contain a great deal of pore space.

An unimpeded drainage hole. Cover the hole with a piece of window screening or similar meshlike material. Don't cover the hole with a piece of broken pot, a stone, or anything similar; doing so negates the purpose of the drainage hole.

A note on "crocking" pots: placing a layer of broken pots, or "crocks," at the bottom of a container to improve drainage is sometimes recommended.

However, a layer of crocks takes up space that could otherwise be filled with more potting mix. This decreases the height of the soil column, which, if taller, would improve drainage (see the next point) while providing more soil volume for the roots.

A layer of crocks can play a useful role at the bottom of a pot lacking a drainage hole: water drains to the bottom of the soil mass and flows into the crocks, providing drained soil to the plant and a reservoir of water for the roots to draw upon (if the roots reach into the crock layer). Also, if you wish to use a particular container (especially a very large one) but believe the plants will not need to grow in a soil mass as large as the volume of the pot, a layer of crocks will reduce the size of the soil mass. Such crocking also provides some stabilizing weight at the bottom of a pot, which helps prevent tall, top-heavy plants from toppling over in wind or under their own unstable weight. If you do use a layer of crocks, place screening, landscape fabric, or other fine-mesh material on top of the crocks before adding the potting mix; the screening prevents, or at least retards, the mix from washing into the crocks and defeating its purpose. Don't use Styrofoam peanuts or similar lightweight material as a bottom layer if you think top-heaviness might pose a problem.

A tall enough soil column (the height of the potting mix) to expedite water movement. To illustrate the physics behind this, place a standard rectangular kitchen sponge

2 Selections of *Sedum, Haworthia,* and *Echeveria* will all thrive in a very well-drained potting mix.

3 These sub-tropical xeric bulbs lie dormant, awaiting spring repotting with fresh cactus mix and water to come alive.

face down on a plate, then saturate it completely. Gently lift it up, keeping one of the two largest faces up until the water stops draining out. Then turn the sponge 90 degrees with one of the two smallest faces up, and notice how much more water drains out. Even though it is still the same sponge, far more water drains out when it is more vertical than horizontal. The identical phenomenon occurs in a potting mix contained in a taller, more vertical pot as opposed to what happens in the same volume of mix in a shorter, more horizontal one: more water drains out of the taller pot than from the shorter one. So the applied physics lesson is this: the taller the soil column, the greater the volume of well-drained soil. Don't take this to an extreme, however, because the taller the pot, the greater its likelihood of toppling over from wind, from an accidental bump, or simply from its own top-heaviness.

THE DIRT ON DIRT

In reality, most commercially available potting mixes will work just fine if they are suitably drained or you add materials to improve drainage. You can also make your own mix from peat, bark, coir, compost, mineral products such as pumice, and even real garden soil—if it works for the plants and you enjoy custom-blending potting mixes, by all means do so. You do not need to use the same mix all the time; as a kid I threw together what was available (within reason, of course) and was usually successful. Keep a few pointers in mind, though:

Commercial mixes can be flexible. Many commercial mixes are the end product of a considerable amount of research (and trial and error), so they suit a huge range of plants.

But commercial mixes can change. The formulas (and product names) for commercial mixes change in response to research and consumer desires. For example, many gardeners prefer a mix that includes coir or bark instead of peat, the use of which raises ecological issues with some people. Be observant of any modifications in mix composition and in your plants' responses to these differences.

Use "real" or garden soil with care. No matter which kind of soil you have in your garden, it won't drain the same way in a pot. Unless your garden soil is quite loose and open, do not use it exclusively in a pot; you may end up with a smelly, sopping wet, poorly drained quagmire. Unsterilized soil may contain virulent organisms that cause rot or other problems. It may also harbor harmful insects and other critters, so buy sterilized soil in bags, or sterilize real soil yourself in an oven or microwave (but hold your nose!). On the plus side, the very small clay or silt particles in garden soil hold more nutrients than the same volume of peat and bark and larger mineral products. Additionally, mixes containing some soil generally lose their structure more slowly than mixes high in peat and other organic materials. This is not important when growing single-season annuals, but it is definitely something to consider for perennials and woody plants.

Good (long-lasting and well-drained) potting mixes are not cheap. It does not, therefore, make much sense to grow short-lived annuals in them if you discard the mix along with the plants at the end of the season. Reuse the mix or opt for a cheaper blend for short-lived plants, and provide the good stuff for plants you intend to keep for more than a season.

Remember physics and engineering. A potting mix has weight and so do water, pots, and plants. Put too much weight on a deck, balcony, roof, or other supported structure, and it will eventually buckle or collapse. You can reduce the weight of a container by using lighter mixes high in organic materials and lighter mineral materials (such as perlite or vermiculite, but not Turface) or by placing a layer of Styrofoam peanuts at the bottom of containers. You can also lessen the load by using pots made of plastic or lighter composite materials instead of terra-cotta, wood, metal, or cast materials, including concrete.

A SPRINKLE A DAY?

Watering: the great mysterious rite of gardening or a simple, straightforward act? It does not need to be puzzling, but it is definitely not an easy, one-size-fits-all proposition either. The basic rule is "Know Your Plants."

This mantra is for every gardener of every stripe. If you do not know the conditions your plants need to thrive, then how can you expect to achieve satisfactory results? Trial and error works sometimes, but do you really want to risk it on a hundred-dollar plant or on your grandmother's heirloom Christmas cactus?

Know Your Plants applies to every aspect of horticulture but is especially critical when it comes to watering, since incorrect watering may well be the principal reason plants fail. Consider this checklist:

Find out the plant's name. You cannot ask a veterinarian questions

④ A specimen of *Lysimachia nummularia* 'Aurea' has been well fertilized and cared for and now needs a larger pot.

about caring for your pet until you let on that Fido is a dog or a snake or a hamster. The same thing goes for plants. Although knowing a plant's full scientific name is not always necessary, the more precise the name, the faster and more accurately you are likely to receive answers about the plant's care. One man's tiger lily is another's *Hemerocallis fulva* or *Lilium lancifolium* or *Solenostemon* (*Coleus*) 'Tiger Lily'.

Ask about a plant's care directly from its source. Ask the salesperson or another employee at the business where you purchased the plant, or look at printed or online information that the nursery or garden shop offers. If you received the plant from a friend, ask them what they know about its care.

Expand your resource base. Consider your next-door neighbor, your local newspaper's gardening columnist, a member of a plant society or garden club, someone from your favorite botanic garden, your local county extension agent, a library, your own bookshelf, the Internet, and wherever else you might be able to find reliable information.

Does the plant have relatives? Try to determine if the new plant is related to another plant or plant group you already have. If so, apply what you know about the similar plant(s) to the new one. Doing so is not a guarantee of success, but at least you have a good chance of being in the ballpark.

Observe what happens. Apply the information you have collected to your own unique gardening conditions and then observe how the plant responds. Plants do not speak, but they certainly respond to the care you provide (or withhold from) them.

Here is another mantra for you: It Depends.

That is often my response when asked "How often do I water it?" or "When do I fertilize it?" or "When should I repot it?" Take, as an example, two begonias of the same type and age; one is planted with several other plants in a large outdoor container on a sunny, exposed patio, while the other ends up as a specimen houseplant on a north-facing windowsill. Should both plants be watered once a week? That frequency might easily result in a dried-up outdoor plant and a root-rotted indoor one. Once you consider all of the variables of a plant's environment, you quickly realize that one size does not fit all.

Your doctor cannot prescribe medication or provide a useful diagnosis until he or she knows as many details as possible about your condition. Likewise, a plant expert will not be able to suggest ways for watering your plant appropriately (or to make any other recommendations, for that matter) until you provide specifics on light, temperature, potting mix, and other factors.

Assuming you know something about a plant and its general watering needs, you can move on to the finer points:

Water the potting mix, not the plants. The roots take up virtually all the plant's water. Dousing a plant may be unavoidable, especially when watering a hundred pots, or may actu-

⑤ 'Gaiety' tulips make an exciting contrast with a *Cordyline australis* 'Albertii', but their growing periods and watering needs differ.

⑥ One size does not fit all, in pot selection and in watering (*Aloc* 'Lizard Lips').

ally be intentional when washing off dust or attempting to eradicate an aphid infestation. In most cases such watering will not cause much damage, but watering the leaves of some plants can provide ideal conditions for disease organisms to flourish (especially late in the day or at night), and drenching the foliage of an overwintering tropical plant in a greenhouse could lead to spotting and leaf drop. Directly and forcefully watering the leaves of succulents with powdery-surfaced foliage (such as some varieties of *Echeveria*) may wash off some of the powder and spoil the look of the plant.

Water from above. Water that evaporates from the surface of a potting mix can leave behind fertilizer salts, the crusty stuff that can also build up on pots, especially ones made of terra-cotta and other porous materials. Watering from above, if possible, helps flush the fertilizer salts back into the ball of potting mix, keeping them off the surface of the mix and the pot. Saucer-watering increases the possibility of salt buildup (because some water will travel up through the soil column and pot, pick up fertilizer salts as it moves, and then leave them behind as it evaporates); if you choose to water from below, be sure to water occasionally from above to reduce the problem.

Don't be overly concerned about water quality. Unless you know for certain your plants are suffering because of it, water quality (such as hardness) should not cause

⑦

⑦ While fiber-optic grass (*Eleocharis montevidensis*) thrives in moist to very wet conditions, it also grows well with less moisture.

⑧ Don't be afraid to add inanimate objects to your container plantings, but make sure they're compatible, such as this small ceramic paired with low-profile succulents.

concern. If your plants are unhappy, have your water tested and follow any recommendations given. Of course, if your research and experience tells you to water certain plants with rainwater or distilled water to avoid problems caused by your usual water supply, then by all means do so.

Does water temperature matter? For most of the container-growing season, probably not, but try not to use icy-cold water on anything that you are overwintering, especially tropicals. Life can be hard enough in winter for them without a cold shock to the roots. And of course never use very hot water.

What about ice cubes? On a related note, some people say to place ice cubes on top of the potting mix so that the melting cubes can slowly release water into the mix. Advocates of this practice argue that placing a few ice cubes on the surface saves time spent on watering and eliminates the mess and bother of carrying around cans or hoses. If it works for you and your plant, by all means use ice to "water" your plants; just keep in mind the caveat about cold water made in the preceding paragraph.

Save time on watering. Here are some ways to shave minutes off your routine: (1) keep your containers within hose reach; (2) have more than one faucet available; (3) buy a long-tubed water wand or similar tool to more easily water hanging baskets or containers beyond arm's reach; (4) group containers together instead of scattering them (but you probably already do this to take advantage of the visual appeal of grouped containers, don't you?); and (5) consider using water-holding gel particles in the potting mix, which work very well if used in the proper amount. Be careful, though: too many gel particles can swell up to the point that their mass heaves plants right out of the pot!

FEED ME

Or more correctly, "fertilize me." Unlike Audrey from *The Little Shop of Horrors,* plants do not actually have mouths, so you cannot really feed them. Instead, several of my college professors and other learned horticulturists compel me to tell you to *fertilize* your plants. Give them fertilizer, not "plant food." Call the method and the material what you will, but Just Do It, another apt mantra to follow.

Very few container-grown plants have the metabolic resources to produce healthy growth and an abundant display of foliage and flowers without an application or two of fertilizer during the growing season. Remember the very first point made in this chapter? Container plants live in a very limited world and cannot depend on a root mass able to search for water and nutrients over a relatively extensive area of soil. Instead, the pot is its world.

So which kind of fertilizer is best?

How much to use? When to apply it? This is another case of It Depends. The mantra applies to fertilizer as much as it does to water and other variables. But here are some general guidelines and some neat tips to help you:

Chemical versus organic. Some gardeners use only "chemical" fertilizers (synthesized or otherwise extensively processed from basic building blocks, such as petroleum and mined minerals), while others swear by "organic" fertilizers (made from materials derived from plants, animals, or minimally processed minerals). Plenty of green thumbs include both types in their programs. Broadly speaking, chemical fertilizers are usually used by plants rather quickly and deliver only what is indicated on the packaging, while organics must be extensively broken down by soil organisms before plants can assimilate them and provide more than what is indicated on the label (including micronutrients and a complex of organic molecules). Know your fertilizers just like you know your plants: ask questions, do your research, and see what works best for you.

Types of fertilizers. Fertilizers are offered in three basic types: granular or powdered, soluble crystals or emulsions, and pelleted (slow release). Chemical fertilizers come in all three types, while organics occur as granular or powdered and emulsions. Chemical fertilizers often have a higher fertilizer analysis (the NPK numbers on the package, indicating the percentages of nitrogen, phosphorus, and potassium) than organics, but some organics offer surprisingly rich analyses.

All three types deliver the goods, but by different delivery systems. Granular and powdered forms must dissolve into the soil water and/or be broken down by microorgan-

⑨

isms. Soluble crystals, when dissolved in water, are almost immediately available to plants, while it takes longer for soil microorganisms to break down emulsions such as fish and seaweed preparations. Pelleted forms require the action of water or heat over time to release their nutrients from the coating material that contains them.

All three types are useful in container gardening, but each has its benefits. Granular and powdered forms are the

cellular structure of the roots. If you choose to use them anyway, consider mulching the surface of the potting mix before applying the fertilizer. The layer of mulch will allow the fertilizer to begin breaking down and become a little less concentrated before reaching the roots.

Water-soluble chemical fertilizers. Miracle-Gro, Peters, and others can be relied on to provide a container plant's diet. Many commercial nurseries use them exclusively, and I have raised many prize-winning container plants solely using these types of fertilizers. Just make sure you are meeting a plant's needs for NPK and the other macro- and micronutrients. Use bloom boosters for flowering plants and those with variegated leaves, and give fertilizers high in nitrogen—even formulations intended for use on lawns—to foliage plants. Try to switch brands occasionally, too.

Organic emulsions. These provide a feast of micronutrients and other valuable substances, but many smell awful until they break down. You might choose not to use them in areas where you and others spend a lot of time, such as near patio dining areas or poolside.

Powdered organics. These may provide nutrients too slowly to benefit annuals, but powdered organic fertilizers are great for perennials and other longer-lived plants. It is difficult to burn the roots with these fertilizers, but they too may smell rather ripe before breaking down. Also, think twice before using some organics if you have dogs or

most economical; soluble crystals and emulsions are conveniently applied during watering; and pelleted types offer the convenience of infrequent application, usually only once or twice per growing season, though they are often the most expensive.

Granular and powdered chemical fertilizers. These may be too hot for plants if they come in direct contact with the roots; they can cause damage by drawing water out of the

⑨ Backlighting emphasizes the glowing health of this *Xanthosoma* 'Lime Zinger'.

⑩ A handful of pelleted fertilizer is often all the food a container planting requires over a growing season.

cats or you suspect the presence of rats nearby—bone meal, blood meal, ground crab shells, and fish meal may attract animals before decomposing. Incorporating organics into the potting mix, applying mulch, and then watering well may discourage curious animals.

Pelleted fertilizers. Some pelleted fertilizers release their contents in response to rising temperatures, while others react to the amount of water surrounding them. Find out the mode of release before using this type: a temperature-dependent fertilizer may be of little or no use in spring or fall (or even summer in some regions), and water-dependent ones will not benefit a cactus that receives very little water.

When should you use fertilizers and how much? Consider the following:

Follow directions and then experiment. Adhere to the package directions initially, but a little experience and experimentation with a given plant will tell you how much more or less to use for the best results. And don't forget to ask questions and do your research.

Enough, but not too much. Some plants—many annuals and tropicals—live fast, die young, and are able to process a great deal of fertilizer during their brief lives. Give them all they can eat during active growth, but make sure not to overindulge them: a wilted plant in apparently moist-enough potting mix may be suffering from fertilizer burn at the roots; rapid salt buildup on the pot is another tip-off.

Growing a giant. If you would like to grow your plants—especially heat-loving annuals and tropicals—to astounding dimensions in one season, mulch the surface of the potting mix with an inch or so of pelleted fertilizer, and then regularly apply water-soluble fertilizers during active growth. Of course, the plants need to be in roomy pots and receive other optimal conditions—don't expect a verbena to grow madly in the shade or a begonia to outdo itself in full sun.

Don't fertilize dormant plants, and go easy on the young. Dormant plants don't need fertilizer, though you can begin applying powdered organic fertilizers toward the end of the dormant season if you want to get a jump on things. Also, don't give young, newly potted plants as much fertilizer as an established specimen of the same kind: step up the fertilizer amount as the plants grow and can handle more. You wouldn't feed a big dinner to a baby or offer only a jar of baby food to a teenager, would you?

Getting rid of the salts. Finally, those annoying, ugly, and potentially damaging crusty salt deposits on pot rims—which can result from using any fertilizer, but especially chemical ones—can usually be scraped off. If they return quickly, you are probably using too much fertilizer, and your plants may be suffering as a result. Watering from above, as discussed in the preceding section, goes a long way toward reducing salt buildup. Also note: salts build up far more rapidly on porous materials, such as terra-cotta and some cast materials, than they do on plastic, resin, and glazed pots.

LET THERE BE LIGHT

Plants live and die by the light they receive—or don't. Without light they cannot engage in photosynthesis, the elegant process that uses energy harnessed from the sun to convert water and carbon dioxide into sucrose, the basic building block of the green world. Some seeds must be exposed to light to germinate, and light directs phototropism, a plant's urge to grow toward the light in search of more. Don't take this essential part of a plant's good health lightly.

Unlike potting mix, water, and fertilizer, you cannot pour light from a bag, add supplements to it, deliver it from a hose or can, make sure it is the right temperature, or choose between chemical and organic varieties. We humans do not play any part in the changing light from season to season, and our only recourse to being unhappy with dark northern winters or blindingly bright southwestern summers is to pack up and move. But you do not need to pay for light, it is inexhaustible, and no one can restrict your access to it (except maybe the neighbor who built a high fence or will not prune his tree).

Happily, you can exert quite a bit of control over the light that brightens your little patch of earth. In fact,

11 All of the succulents in this planting thrive in bright window light, which captures their varied colors and textures.

as a container gardener you have the edge over in-ground gardeners, who cannot move a sun-baked pansy or a light-starved geranium as easily and quickly as you can, because your plants grow in portable packages.

This brings us to another container-gardening mantra: Move It.

If you decide, based on observations guided by thoughtful research, that a container planting might grow more happily on the patio along the east side of your house instead of by the south-facing front door, then move it. Is your pot of ornamental peppers looking a bit tall and thin in its spot behind the tomatoes? Move it. Even on the smallest deck or balcony, moving a pot from one side to the other or rearranging the placement within a group of pots can produce dramatic results.

Remember the mantra Know Your Plants. It applies to their light needs as much as any other factor, so do your research before situating any planted container in your garden or

12 Tucked against a protective shingled wall, this planting of fuchsia, golden *Heliochrysum*, nasturtiums, and green cordyline blooms luxuriously.

on the deck. You must also know your light—specifically, where the sun comes up and where it sets (an easy task) and how its quality and intensity change over the course of a year (much harder) in your garden. Where are the shadowy cool spots of spring? In which part of the garden does the noonday midsummer sun turn from giver of life to dryer of potting mix and scorcher of foliage? Your beautiful maidenhair fern may thrive on the patio in spring but might look like corn flakes in the same spot in summer.

Don't go crazy trying to find the perfect spot, however. Many plants show a remarkable adaptability to light conditions, and some exhibit different characteristics depending on light exposure, which you as a container gardener can fully exploit. The foliage of *Alocasia* 'Black Velvet' turns an almost iridescent black in full sun, but specimens of the same variety take on a rich, dark green coloration in partial shade. Many coleus show different colors and patterns in sun versus shade; you can get an idea of what a coleus grown in sun might look like in shade by examining the leaves in the shaded center of the plant or on the lower parts out of direct sun. And, of course, the quantity of blooms a flowering plant produces depends on the light it receives. You might like the more modest look of a shade-grown hydrangea over the flashy abundance of one luxuriating in full sun. In the long run, a slightly stretched-out or denser-than-normal plant might appeal to you more than one with a textbook appearance.

Here are a few aspects of light to keep in mind:

The plant's point of view. A spot that seems quite bright to you probably seems like a dimly lit room to some plants, especially many cacti and succulents, which grow natively in areas that receive enormous amounts of very strong sunlight. Keep an eye peeled for loss of color, thin leaves, growth that looks stretched out, and poor or no flowering on any plant that you know requires plenty of sun to do well. If a plant is doing poorly, remember the mantra Move It.

Backlighting. Take advantage of the magical effects created by light shining through, not on, a plant, particularly in late summer and into autumn. Every leaf peeper who travels the highways to enjoy the fall colors knows that a backlit red maple or golden quaking aspen makes more of an impression than the same species lit from the front.

Shadows. Sunlight produces shadows, and shadows produce drama. Their darkness and length change as the seasons progress, providing another opportunity for creating memorable container-garden compositions. Even the pots can interact here; tall pots cast longer shadows than short ones, and you can watch their shadows move throughout the day, much as you might look at a sundial.

GOING HOT AND COLD

As with light, there is not a whole lot a container gardener can do about the overall daily, seasonal, and annual temperature conditions in the garden, short of moving to a warmer or cooler place. A savvy gardener can deal with the effects of heat and cold by employing some techniques and tricks, though.

First, a refresher on some basics of how plants relate to temperature and its ups and downs:

Temperature range. Plants are genetically programmed

to survive within two points of a given temperature range. Tropical plants are adapted to the higher end of the range but cannot withstand freezing temperatures; and some perish well before the thermometer drops to 32°F (0°C). Tundra natives tolerate temperatures well below 0°F (18°C) but may suffer in 80°F (27°C) heat. Within its own two particular extremes, every plant has an optimal temperature range in which it will grow, flower, and set seed, but the range is not always the same for every process. That is why a container gardener in Minnesota can grow a banana tree as a big, leafy specimen in summer, but it will probably never flower and make fruit: the plant just does not receive enough heat. This also explains why many cacti and other succulents never flower for anyone who brings them in before the cold weather arrives. The plants survive with the help of the higher temperatures indoors, but they never bloom because the absence of sufficiently cold temperatures prevents the plants from setting flower buds.

Plants' survival strategies. Many plants have their own internally determined methods for surviving temperature extremes in their native habitats. For example, trees and shrubs may drop their leaves, perennials often die back to a crown, and other plants disappear aboveground and spend the unfavorable period underground as a bulb, corm, or other resting structure. Others, including many cacti and other succulents, simply slow down their metabolic engines for the duration of the hard times. While such dormant states are often triggered by temperature, moisture and light levels also play a part, bringing us to another gardening mantra: Let It (sort of) Be.

When a plant is dormant, let it sleep, at least for a while.

It needs its rest to be able to grow well the following season. Of course gardeners are often unwilling to let plants always go about their natural ways; think of the practices of pruning and growing plants in pots, for starters. We have some methods at our disposal to manipulate dormancy, such as bulb forcing, overwintering actively growing tropicals in heated greenhouses, and restricting or providing water for cacti and succulents. All of these methods allow gardeners to bend the laws of nature without breaking them, though, occasionally, in our often uninformed zeal we exceed the bounds of nature and inevitably kill the plants.

Know Your Plants applies to temperature as much as it does to water, fertilizer, and light, so do your research before adopting a summer-dormant succulent or a spring-blooming camellia that must experience some winter cold to bloom well. And as you become familiar with your plants, you may discover ways to play with their specific requirements to prevent them from going completely dormant.

Next, let's look at how temperature basics apply to container gardening. Here are a few ways to garden sensibly within the temperature conditions available to you or to take advantage of special spots in your garden:

When to move a plant outside. Don't attempt to grow plants outside in containers until the air temperature is suitable and any danger of frost has passed. Try to resist the temptation to buy annuals and tropicals too early in the season, unless you can keep them in a greenhouse, on a sun porch, in a garage, or on a windowsill until it is safe to plant

⓭ Make sure nighttime temperatures are warm enough before placing potted agapanthus and eucomis outside.

them outside. If you do not have a protected spot indoors, keep the plants near a south-facing wall and cover them with horticultural fleece, old bed sheets, or very light blankets at night if cold temperatures or light frost are forecast. Tie the covers down in a few spots if you expect light wind. Avoid using newspaper, which blows away easily, and plastic, which can conduct damaging cold temperatures onto a plant's leaves.

Overwintering. If you intend to keep container plants from one season to the next, consider the conditions you can provide for them. Hardy trees, shrubs, and perennials need a cold winter dormancy to grow well the following season, so bury plant and pot in a protected spot of your garden; or tip the pot over and cover plant and pot with leaves or burlap; or surround the pot with horticultural fleece; or overwinter the plants in or out of their pots in a cold frame or unheated garage. The plants will sleep until spring's alarm clock wakes them, and then you will need to resume actively caring for them. Tender plants must be kept warm enough to maintain them somewhere along the

spectrum of actively growing, semidormant, or dormant, so windowsills, light carts, heated basements, or sun porches and greenhouses can be pressed into service.

Keep an eye on your plants' watering needs, depending on their activity: growing plants need far more than dormant ones. Even dormant plants can benefit from a dribble of water once in a while to prevent them from drying out completely, but do not start dribbling until the plants look slightly shriveled. Gradually increase watering for all of your overwintered tender plants as the days get longer and the temperatures rise, including plants growing under timed lights in a consistently maintained temperature. Their internal clocks are ticking too, waiting for the time to resume active growth.

Microclimates. Discover and exploit any microclimates you have in your garden. The area near a south-facing house wall, fence, or flight of stone steps generally warms up fastest in spring, so you can start gardening in that spot sooner than you can near a north-facing wall, which warms up last. A south-facing inside corner near the house or fence will also warm up more quickly, but it can also become a blast furnace in summer, so use that spot to push heat-loving tropicals to their limits of growth and flowering.

Areas at the base of a hill or on the uphill side of a fence or dense hedge allow cooler air to gather. This can be a bad thing in spring and fall, since frost pockets may occur in these areas and cut a plant's life short or prevent a late bloomer from providing fall's last hurrah. On the other hand, the slightly cooler air in a lower area can prolong the life of cool-season annuals, such as pansies and diascias. The high shade of trees also reduces air temperature, as does a big umbrella or roof overhang.

Dark-colored surfaces—such as patios and decks—become hotter in sunlight than lighter-colored ones and can heat up potting mix to dangerous temperatures. Raise heat-sensitive plants slightly off the surface with bricks, flat stones, or pot feet to cool things down a bit. Alternately, you can deliberately place heat lovers directly onto such a surface to raise the soil temperature. You can even create your own microclimate within a group of containers: the potting mix in pots on the sunny edges of a grouping will be considerably warmer than the mix in the pots behind other pots or shaded by neighboring plants.

Cooling things down. Suppose you have a favorite dark-colored container, especially a big one such as a concrete planter or cast-iron urn. You know it will absorb heat in summer, which might damage roots, but you have the perfect sun-loving plant for the container. How can you reduce the temperature of the potting mix so that you can have it all?

Place the plant into a simple terra-cotta or plastic pot at least two inches smaller in diameter than the dark pot. Place some coarse gravel at the bottom of the dark pot, then center the planted pot within the larger dark one. Loosely stuff any of the following between the two pots: Styrofoam peanuts, bubblewrap, fiberglass insulation, woodchips, coarsely ground corncobs, pine needles, or anything else that will hold the inner pot in place and provide plenty of temperature-modulating air spaces.

14   The shallow pool creates its own microclimate, a comfortably moist home for *Cyperus papyrus* amid the arid landscape.

Moistening any organic material occasionally will reduce the temperature a bit more: as the water evaporates, it absorbs heat from its surroundings and cools the air and the pots—and in turn the potting mix. Just make sure the larger container has a drainage hole; if it lacks one, be very careful not to add so much water that the mix and plant roots remain in standing water.

You can use this pot-within-a-pot, or cachepot, technique for any combination of containers. Hide an ugly or plain pot within a beautiful Della Robbia-style container, glazed oriental-motif urn, undrained lead planter, rustic wicker basket, antique washtub, or any other container you wish.

OTHER CULTURAL FACTORS
Wind
While gentle breezes rustling the leaves and cooling a sweaty brow play a part in the idyllic garden dream, gusting, destructive winds take a starring role in a gardener's worst nightmare. Air movement of any kind

⑮ Resting on thin stems, the blooms of *Anemonella thalictroides* 'Oscar Schoaf' require extra care and protection.

exerts a drying effect on plants as well as on the potting mix in containers, so while some stirring of the air is a good thing (it helps reduce the severity of mildew, for example), air movement for too long and with too much force behind it can lead to grief.

Protect your plants. Site your containers in a protected spot near the house, a fence, or a hedge.

Anchor your pots. Place a layer of gravel or rocks at the bottom of containers to provide increased stability in the face of wind, but remember to keep any drainage hole(s) unimpeded.

Cluster your pots. Group containers closely together to support each other.

Secure hanging plants. Use sturdy, well-secured hardware to suspend hanging baskets.

Pay attention to watering. Keep a close eye on watering needs, especially in breezy spots such as porches and breezeways between buildings.

Choose different plants. Grow shorter, more compact plants with small or narrow leaves. They are more stable in wind and less prone to shredding than tall, top-heavy plants with large leaves that act like sails (if they do not get torn apart first).

Support

Unless you want them to trail down the sides of a pot, dangle from a hanging basket, or weave through other plants, climbing plants must be given some kind of support. Whether you use an elegant wrought-iron tuteur or a simple teepee of bamboo stakes and twine, keep these points in mind:

Secure the support firmly in the container. If the support has no legs to push into the potting mix, anchor it with long U-shaped pins pressed firmly into the mix, routinely checking that the support remains anchored.

Anticipate stability problems. A bare support at the beginning of the season will offer relatively little resistance to the wind, but as the plants cover it the increased surface area may eventually become an easy target for toppling.

Check your supports over time. Organic materials deteriorate, particularly in moist potting mix. Check your supports for rot and other damage every now and then, especially at the beginning of the season. Don't expect the base of bamboo or wood structures to last for more than a couple of seasons unless treated.

Choose attractive supports. Choose simpatico supports that combine attractively with your plants and containers. You will be looking at the supports all season, after all, and even if a plant eventually covers the support completely, you will still need to wait for that to happen.

Plant Problems

Recommendations for dealing with pests, diseases, and other problems are the stuff of many a newspaper and magazine article, county extension–office brochure, and reference book, so by all means take advantage of such resources available to you. What follows is the rationale and basic process of Integrated Pest Management (IPM), a comprehensive method that enables you to determine how best to deal with a problem should it arise.

1. Identify what is causing the damage by thinking like a doctor. What are the symptoms? Are the leaves wilting?

Are stems broken? Are flowers sparse or absent? Then determine how many different agents can cause the problem. For example, a plant may wilt in response to a bacterial infection, borers tunneling in the stems, dry potting mix, excessive cold or heat, or rotten roots. If you believe you can identify the cause, go to step 2. If you are not certain or suspect more than one culprit, do some research and ask questions of your resource people before moving on.

2. Decide if the damage is severe enough to take action. Does the wilting appear on just one branch, or does it occur all over the plant? Are other plants affected? Is it occurring on a valuable plant or on one of a hundred? If the damage is minor and does not seem to be worsening or spreading, or if the patient is easily replaceable, then your best options may be to do nothing or to discard the plant. If you think the problem requires a remedy, move on to step 3.

3. Determine appropriate methods for control and remedy. Then begin with the method that poses the smallest risk to you and others, including your pets, the patient, any nearby plants, and the environment. Maybe all the patient needs is some water. If it soon wilts again, consider repotting it to give it more root room, or move it to a shadier, less windy spot. If your attempted remedy fails, consider another possible cause and appropriate course of action.

4. Don't impulsively reach for a pesticide or other chemical solution. Maybe all you need to do is stick a wire into that hole in the stem to kill the borer inside or prune off the one wilting stem to bring the problem to an end. If you must use chemicals, begin with the least toxic ones (such as soaps and oils for insect problems). If they do not produce a satisfactory result, go to the next level of strength. As you proceed up the chemical ladder, ask yourself if the potency of the attempted cure and the risks it poses are in line with the severity of the problem and the value of the plant.

5. Continue pursuing all options until the problem is resolved. Keep in mind that as you are treating the

16 The vividly colored daisies of *Senecio confusus* appear vigorous when climbing strong supports.

17 Certainly beautiful for a time, the flower stalks of *Begonia* 'Art Hodes' are best removed after the flowers fade.

patient the pest may go away, weather conditions may change, or you may decide the plant is not worth all the fuss and bother after all.

An ounce of prevention is worth a pound of cure. The following actions will help greatly in the battle against plant problems:

Choose pest- and disease-resistant plants. Plenty of plants are naturally more capable of withstanding problems than others. Plant breeders and nurseries constantly offer new selections that may be more resistant than the ones you are currently growing and coddling.

Provide optimal conditions to the best of your ability. Optimal conditions promote healthy growth. Of course a

caterpillar will still feed on a perfectly healthy plant, but the plant will be better able to bounce back from the removal of some leaves than a stressed one.

Practice garden sanitation. Remove badly infested or diseased plants, pull weeds that may harbor insects, and discard dead plants at the end of the season.

Interact with your plants. Above all, get out in your garden and interact with your plants. While tending their needs and admiring their beauty, you might spot a problem in its early, more easily controllable stage.

Pruning, Pinching, and Deadheading

No, these are not the English translations of the names for the mythological Three Fates. These terms relate to "editing" plant parts for the benefit of the whole. "Pruning" means the removal of a plant part for any number of reasons: thinning suckers, taking out broken or diseased branches, raising the crown of a tree by cutting off the lowest ring of branches, shearing hedges, trimming topiary, and maybe even cutting a climber back to the ground to rejuvenate it. "Pinching" (sometimes called "stopping") refers specifically to removing young shoot tips to promote increased branching. "Deadheading" means removing spent flowers to improve the appearance of a plant and to direct a plant's energies into producing more growth (and maybe more flowers) instead of forming seeds.

Container plants benefit from pruning, pinching, and deadheading just as much as—if not more than—plants growing in the open ground. Since a container plant has a finite amount of resources to draw upon, limiting its growth can help prevent repeated drying out, spindly

growth, or sparse flowering resulting from less than optimal levels of water or fertilizer. Also, since container plants may be viewed more closely and more often than plants in the open ground, pruning, pinching, and deadheading keep them looking their best and within their container proportions.

Here are a few tips on these methods:

Consider delaying your gratification. Even though you may be able to buy small annual plants already in bloom, such as petunias, angelonias, and sages, resist the temptation to leave the flowers on the plants for your immediate enjoyment. Pinching many plants immediately after you plant them will result in increased branching and more flowers down the road. If you have nerves of steel, pinch them again after they have put on a few inches of growth; this will produce an even more colorful plant down the line. You decide which form of gratification you want from your purchases: immediate, which might lead to plants burning out in the height of the season, or delayed, which keeps you waiting longer for a more impressive and satisfying display.

Definitely delay your gratification sometimes. Some plants require pinching to be enjoyed at their best, especially those grown strictly for their foliage. Be sure to pinch coleus, alternantheras, iresines, plectranthus, and basils early, and be prepared to do it another time or two before letting the plants grow out naturally.

To deadhead or not to deadhead. You can drive yourself to distraction deadheading some heavily blooming plants that just don't need it. Fanflowers, marigolds, and verbenas, for example, should continue to bloom heavily even without being deadheaded, and can you imagine trying to remove the spent flowers of impatiens? On the other hand, fruiting plants, most notably ornamental peppers, must not be deadheaded if you want to enjoy their fruit display (and of course you do), while heliotropes, repeat-blooming hydrangeas, and geraniums require routine deadheading to keep them looking presentable.

Giving plants breathing room. Overzealous plants, particularly tropicals, can be judiciously deleafed to prevent them from swamping their pot companions. If your canna, banana, or brugmansia looks like it is elbowing out its more reserved neighbors, removing a few leaves will open up some space and slow the brutes down a little. This is not the remedy for planting King Kong and Jiminy Cricket together in the same pot, however. Try to roughly match plant vigor when planning your containers, or at least segregate plants to separated areas in a large pot to give each plant its space. You might also consider growing the bountiful plant in one pot and the more timid in another and then placing them next to each other.

Weeding, Mulching, and Topdressing

If you routinely water and fertilize your potted plants, weeds will make the most of those ideal conditions and rapidly proliferate. Of course you want to weed your container plantings; vigorous weeds can quickly overwhelm small plants, and most weeds spoil the good looks of your efforts. Applying a mulch will help suppress weeds, will slow

⑱ A topdressing can hide a multitude of sins, such as white spots of perlite or tiny weeds, and provide a pleasing transition between the textures of plant and pot.

water evaporation from the potting mix, and will prevent water from splashing onto your plants during rainstorms or watering. A topdressing provides the same benefits of mulch; it is just a fancier way to cover the mix. Topdressings such as gravel, pebbles, or coarse sand provide a neat, clean look and will not decompose like mulches do.

Keep the following in mind when applying these techniques:

Weeds can be beautiful, too. Some weeds might actually contribute to the good looks of your container plantings, at least until they grow too large or begin to deteriorate. If you know a weed will stay small, look good for a while, and not produce a trillion seeds before it dies, why not let it be?

Light versus dark. Light-colored mulches reflect the sun's rays, while darker ones absorb them. Use a lighter mulch to help reduce the surface temperature of the potting mix in summer, and apply a darker one in spring to warm the mix and give young plants a boost.

Close planting eliminates or greatly reduces the need for mulch.

Reserve topdressings for specimen plants. Trees and shrubs (including tropicals) with nothing growing at their feet, as well as many cacti and other succulents, look their best against the attractive, neutral background that topdressing provides. Look for topdressings at pet-supply stores in the aquarium section as well as at agricultural- and building-supply stores. Make sure to bring along a pair of strong arms and a good back when buying topdressings in quantity—they are rocks, after all, and even a small bag is rather heavy.

When You Can't Be There for Them

What can you do to provide for your plants' needs when you are away? Like everything else in gardening, the answer depends on many factors, including the number of pots, the season and weather, the length of your absence, and the plants' needs. If you will be gone for more than a few days in the middle of summer, for example, consider asking a gardening friend or even a professional service to tend your plants. However, if you expect your absence to be short, you might want to employ these tricks:

Move it. Move sun-grown plantings into shade or

(19) Three resident echeverias are being pulled apart to occupy a larger container; this is a good time to examine the root structure for mealy bugs.

(20) You can't take the *Muscari* 'Valerie Finnis' with you, so water well before leaving town.

to the north side of the house, and place small pots on the surface of the potting mix underneath large plants.

Prewater. Put saucers under the pots and water the containers from above until the saucers are full.

Mulch. Surround smaller, shorter pots with mulch and water the mulch as well as the pots before you depart.

Install a drip-watering system. This is a good idea even when you are not away for an extended period. A system of tubes, with outlets in every pot that can benefit from the same watering schedule, saves time as well as water, whether used in five pots or fifty. If you do not like the looks of the tubes, there are plenty of ways to hide the system within a group of containers or disguised under mats, mulch, or plants.

Board plants with a friend or at a local nursery.

Take plants with you. A long-time friend of mine spends her summers hundreds of miles from home, and she loads up her car with smaller, needier container plants that she can tend all summer. The larger, less demanding plants remain at home under a friend's care.

CONTAINER CHECKLIST

Before you start planting, review the following checklist. Going through it in advance might save you time in the long run.

1. Which basic conditions does a given site provide?
   - Is there enough room to accommodate the container without it getting in the way of everyday traffic?
   - Is a water source nearby?
   - Are the light conditions right for the type of plants you plan on placing here?
   - Is the site protected or exposed?
   - Is it in a spot that allows for easy routine maintenance?
2. What is the effect you want to achieve from each individual pot?
   - Is it going to hold a specimen plant or be a combination pot?
   - Will the pot be paired with other pots and objects?
   - What are your specific desires regarding color, line, form, space, and texture?
   - Will the pot serve as a focal point?
   - Will the plant(s) be complemented by the pot or simply contained by it?
3. Do you want the pot to provide a season-long display or simply be enjoyed during a specific event?
   - Which design elements do you wish to enjoy for the entire season?

21 These pots are no more than ten inches tall, but they demonstrate the proportions of a long tom. This pot form provides an easy way to grow and display sensitive or delicate plants, such as the *Lewisia* seen here.

- Do you want to put considerable effort and money into a short-term pot?

4. Which plants will provide what you are looking for?
   - If you are considering a combination pot, will all of the plants grow well together?
   - Might something other than a container planting (garden art, inground planting, fence, or hedge) meet your needs?

5. Where can you most cost-effectively obtain the plants and supplies (pots, potting mix, supports, fertilizer, mulch, and topdressing) that you will need?

6. Do you want immediate gratification, or can you wait?
   - If immediate gratification is the answer, are larger/blooming/already trained plants available?
   - If you can wait for a fuller display, do you know how and when to pinch back the plants, fertilize them, and provide other care?

7. When can you put the planting together and place it outside?
   - Is frost protection an issue? If so, after which date can the plants remain outside?
   - Will you need help moving the finished pot if you don't compose it on site?

8. Are you prepared to deal with problems, including pests and diseases, care in your absence, winterizing, and weather damage?

Always keep in mind the mature sizes and forms of the plants as you arrange them in the pot. In general, position bigger and taller plants (and climbers that will grow upward) in the center or back, and smaller plants (and climbers that will hang over the edge of the pot, plus any trailers) to the outside and front.

Also as a general guideline, when planting in place, position trellises (and other tall and/or bulky supports with parts that need to go deeply into the potting mix) as you add the layers of mix, and then plant around the supports. Teepees and other supports with shallower bases and many aboveground parts are better placed once you have positioned the plants, especially if you are putting several plants within the support. If not planting in place, remember that you will need to carefully jockey both the pot and the support as you move the container. That said, try to plant in place any pot that includes tall or bulky supports.

Hanging Baskets and Strawberry Jars

The same planting procedure applies to wire hanging baskets as for on-ground pots, with an exception or two. It is helpful to place the basket on a bucket, washtub, or other container to prevent the basket from rolling around as you work with it. Also, don't add the chains or other hanging device until the basket is fully planted. If you plan on planting the underside of a basket you must do this in place, especially if the finished basket will be even remotely heavy. Wire hanging baskets require a liner of some type, such as one made from compressed fiber or moss, or you can hand-stuff sphagnum moss between the wires. Add the liner and then some potting mix, which you should gently firm down. Cut slits in the liner and insert the lowest plants. Placing the root balls in paper cones or plastic bags can help as you push the root balls through the liner and into the mix. Repeat the process until the underside is done, and then plant the top.

Planting strawberry jars is essentially the same as planting regular containers, but with a twist. You must plant in stages: begin by placing the screening and ballast (optional) at the bottom, and then add some potting mix and gently firm it to just below the level of the lowest pocket(s). Place plants in the pockets, and then push mix around the roots and into the center of the jar. Repeat the procedure until you have planted all of the pockets, then continue as you would with a standard pot. Some friendly advice: don't fill the entire pot with potting mix before attempting to plant it; you'll end up pushing mix out the sides and top and may find it very difficult to position the roots in the jar. Also, floppy plants and those with few roots can be held in place with wires bent into long U-shaped pins pushed well into the mix.

22 Container plants don't necessarily look their best when placed in the ground or suspended in air. Chairs, tables, and other garden furniture can make novel settings for your plants.

11: choosing a pot

Perhaps you are asking yourself, "What is there to choosing a pot? Pots are pots, aren't they?" Or maybe you are reading this before the chapters on the elements of design in Part 1, which demonstrate that pots can play a very important role in the overall appearance of a container planting. Regardless, I hope you will see that there are plenty of considerations to ponder when choosing a pot.

A world of choices exists out there, and it pays to do some thinking and research before selecting a container. Before exploring specific materials, here are some important basics to consider:

Know Your Plants. The previous chapter introduced this mantra, and it applies to choosing pots as well. Don't forget the basic requirements of your plants, especially their need for movement of water and air within the potting mix. Some pot materials allow water and air to pass through them, promoting drainage in the mix but also accelerating water loss. Most plants benefit from the presence of a drainage hole; if lacking one, most containers can be drilled to make one. Don't try to make one with a chisel or similar tool unless you are very adept; you will probably end up cracking the pot in the process. Also, consider the volume of potting mix that can be contained within a pot. Don't try to grow a big (or potentially big) plant in a too-small pot, and avoid putting plants that stay small into a large volume of mix. The latter wastes money on excess

mix, and mix at the bottom of the pot may go "sour" (basically rotten and smelly) if no roots penetrate it, especially during the heat of summer.

Avoid "waisted" pots (containers with constrictions somewhere below the top of the pot), except for annuals and other plants you intend to grow for only one season. Also think twice about using those with sides that taper out toward the bottom. It is almost impossible to remove a plant from such containers when the time comes to repot them, short of plunging a knife straight down into the root mass and around it to free it. You might slice off quite a few important roots in the process. This recommendation does not apply to annuals and other plants that are discarded at the end of the season.

Consider the relative permanence of the pot material. Choose more durable materials for longer-lived plants, especially topiaries and large plants that may stay in the same container for years. Plants with briefer lives can also be planted in antique lead containers or high-fired terracotta, but less durable clay, plastic, and untreated wood make fine choices if you do not want to invest in longer-lasting materials.

Consider cost. You could spend anywhere from a few cents to a few thousand dollars or more on a pot. Cost goes up with the value of a pot's basic constituents and the potential life span of its material, so decide if you want to make (and can afford) the investment in costlier materials. Over time, more expensive pots may save you some money you would otherwise spend on replacing cheaper ones. Some less expensive materials, including reconstituted stone and fiberglass, convincingly copy the look of

① While you may not have a wall of pots to choose from, it's a good idea to keep a selection of various shapes, sizes, and materials on hand.

stone tend to be less forgiving than plastic, resins, wood, and metal.

Consider weight. Finally, an extremely practical matter to consider: how much weight can you manage without help? Even relatively large pots made of plastic and fiberglass weigh little, but the moist potting mix and the plant(s) they contain add many pounds. A small stone trough or lead planter may be more than you can lift, even without the mix and plants. Dollies and carts are certainly helpful, but you still need to get the containers onto them, move everything to the display or storage spot, and then put the containers into place. You might consider permanently leaving heavier containers in a given spot. Also, if you garden on a deck, roof, or balcony, you must give careful thought and planning to the combined weight of all the containers you tend. One positive attribute of heavy pots is their greater stability in

② A simple incised motif adds interest to an empty pot, but will it complement or detract from the living contents?

③ Glazed clay pots offer limitless possibilities— shape, color, surface texture, and the reflective quality of the finish.

their far costlier stone, terra-cotta, and lead counterparts.

Consider what freezing weather will do to a pot. Anyone who gardens in areas that experience freezing temperatures needs to understand frost and cold resistance (and the lack of it). Very porous materials, including unglazed clay and wood, absorb and retain water, which expands when it freezes. That leads to cracking and flaking, both of which can destroy a container or, at the very least, spoil attractive surface features such as fluting or sculpted ornamentation. Don't expose pots made from less resistant

materials to the elements during winter; bring them inside, or at least cover them in place with plastic or other nonporous material. Weather-resistant pots may be left outside during winter, but if in doubt bring a container inside for storage out of the snow and rain.

Consider sturdiness. Although some pot materials are sturdier than others, try to avoid banging and otherwise knocking around any container. A trowel can crack some pots if carelessly used, and smacking one pot into another will often chip or crack both. Porous materials and

wind, which comes in handy when growing large and top-heavy tropicals, trees, and shrubs, and standard topiaries.

CLAY

Clay containers—ranging from everyday, inexpensive, machine-made pots to one-of-a-kind, pricey, handmade treasures—are probably the most popular choice for container gardeners. Look for the fairly thick-walled, darker-toned pots; those with thinner walls and brighter coloration may be more apt to break from careless or rough handling and freezing winter conditions. The effects of cold weather can destroy or damage clay pots in one season, as water held within the clay expands as it freezes, leading to cracking and flaking. Handmade clay pots can provide more character by virtue of their nonstandard shapes and often mellower, earthier colors. Unglazed clay allows water and air to pass through it, while glazed clay greatly restricts their movement. However, the huge range of colors and intriguing shapes of glazed pots open up a world of creative possibilities, and the glaze usually provides greater

resistance to winter damage. When in doubt about a container's weather resistance, cover or store it in a shed, garage, or basement during freezing weather.

TERRA-COTTA

A terra-cotta pot is made from essentially the same material as a clay pot, but terra-cotta is fired in the kiln at higher temperatures. Being stronger and far more waterproof than regular clay, terra-cotta provides much greater resistance to winter damage. Its coloration is usually less raw-looking (more subtle) than clay, and its often-present whitish coating when new and tendency to age attractively add to terra-cotta's more refined appearance. Less expensive terra-cotta pots are machine-made but usually hold up almost as well as the more expensive handmade ones. The difference, of course, is in the artistry; highly skilled craftspeople create elegantly simple to highly ornate terra-cotta containers by hand, and thousands of dollars can change hands over one large pot. If cared for properly, your grandchildren can inherit your terra-cotta pots (if not your green thumb!).

WOOD

Almost any kind of wood, from the most basic pine to the rarest tropical hardwood, can be used to make simple homemade boxes, rustic-looking whiskey barrels, high-end Versailles planters, and one-of-a-kind organic shapes. All wood will rot over time in the presence of water and soil micro-organisms (not to mention carpenter ants and termites), but some hard-woods and chemically treated soft-woods can last a remarkably long time if properly maintained. Try to raise wooden containers off the soil or other surfaces on bricks, stones, or pot feet; line them with plastic or metal; protect them from the ravages of winter (as with clay, water in wood expands as it freezes, often causing damage); and consider storing them empty for winter. A coat of paint and/or wood preservative helps too, but be careful with preservatives: some are toxic to plants, particularly right after

④ A mellow weathered teak box provides a gentle setting for this soft composition of *Hebe buxifolia* 'Variegata', *Scaevola aemula*, and *Ipomoea batatas* 'Blackie.'

⑤ Picture a pale purple viola or a few yellow crocuses in one of these cans, and you'll understand the appeal of a gray metal cachepot.

application. Be aware that some tropical hardwoods are harvested from diminishing wild sources, while others are plantation-raised, providing a far more sustainable supply.

METAL

Iron, steel, aluminum, copper, zinc, and lead vessels add a distinctive touch to any container planting. Wrought and cast iron evoke elegant gardens of centuries past or perhaps, depending on the design, twenty-first-century modern ones. Iron rusts, so painting it can protect it from water. Stainless steel will not rust, and pieces made from it can be used as stylish, industrial-looking cachepot covers for less attractive pots. Aluminum weighs much less than most metals but will quickly develop a white surface coating, which is appealing to some and not to others. New and polished copper cast a warm glow, and aged (patinaed) copper offers mellow shades of green and brown. Zinc can be cut into rather thin and lightweight sheets that can be shaped into useful cachepots; like most metals, it develops a surface character over time. Aristocratic lead containers conventionally decorate stately old country homes but can look equally appropriate in more modern settings. Be very careful with lead: its weight can crush a toe, and it deforms very easily when handled or bumped.

PLASTIC

Don't let stereotypical notions of plastic prevent you from gardening with pots made from it. While most plastic pots are widely considered plain-looking or maybe even vulgar, some plastics closely copy the look of clay, terra-cotta, wood, metal, and stone and cost far less than their counterparts. You can always cachepot a less attractive plastic pot inside a more elegant one. Some plants, especially those that like a moister potting mix, benefit from a plastic pot's ability to hold water longer. Thicker plastic pots hold up better to physical abuse than thin-walled ones, but be aware that many plastics, no matter how sturdy, gradually decompose in the presence of the ultraviolet light that is a natural part of sunshine, becoming brittle (or at the very least developing unsightly faded areas). That solid-looking plastic pot may shatter or crumble when you try to lift it after exposure to the sun for a season or two. Look for plastic pots with an ultraviolet-light inhibitor added.

RESINS

A catchall term for several plastic-like materials, resins look and behave much like many plastics but often hold up better in sunlight and take more physical abuse than plastics. Resins can be dyed to mimic other materials as well.

STONE

Nothing looks as solid and ageless as stone, whether roughly hewn or highly polished. A stone container presents a visually exciting contrast to its organic contents and surroundings. Stone can be carved into simple shapes or highly ornamented pieces of

⑥ A metal container adds both figurative and literal weight to a planting: Before using one, make sure you can manage the combined weight of it and its contents.

⑦ A stone trough such as this can provide a timeless, even ancient touch to a garden.

sculpted elegance, and it withstands physical abuse and winter conditions far better than many materials. However, even small stone containers may present a weight-management problem to young or less robust gardeners, and they are not cheap: a handsomely weathered, antique stone trough can set you back thousands of dollars. New stone troughs are being produced in China and India, and while not inexpensive, they cost much less than their highly prized peers. Here is a tip: to make a rough-surfaced, new stone container look much older, brush it with buttermilk, live-culture yogurt, or manure tea (manure "steeped" in water a few days) during warm weather; then place the container in a shady spot (and preferably planted). Moisten it occasionally and soon algae will begin to grow, eventually followed by mosses, ferns, and perhaps even self-

8 Ornate adornments aren't just for terra-cotta anymore; plastic, resin, and composite pots also often feature such detail.

9 A thoughtfully placed composition of beautiful containers don't even need living plants to make an impression.

sowed seedlings of nearby garden plants. This also works on clay and reconstituted stone as well as on terra-cotta, but often more slowly.

RECONSTITUTED STONE/COMPOSITES

Grind stone up and bind it together with cement, epoxy, or similar glues and a dye. The resulting reconstituted stone can be cast into shapes, avoiding the effort, time, and expense of carving an intact block of stone. Good-quality reconstituted stone closely mimics the appearance and weight of natural stone, but it may be less tolerant of physical abuse and weather conditions. It is certainly less costly.

CONCRETE

Similar to reconstituted stone in its versatility, appearance, and weight, concrete usually costs less than stone. Dark, smooth-surfaced concrete planters combine beautifully with just about any plant, but keep a close eye on dark concrete in sun: the surface can heat up enough to almost cook plant roots (for ways to deal with this, see page 135).

HYPERTUFA

Justly beloved by rock gardeners, hypertufa combines the porosity of clay with the good looks of stone and the value of concrete, and you can make hypertufa containers at home. Yet don't think that only delicate and difficult alpine gems make the only worthy tenants of a hypertufa container. Moisture-loving plants as well as many trees and shrubs look and grow beautifully in hypertufa, as do many cacti and other succulents. And no one is preventing you from growing annuals and tropicals in them.

FIBERGLASS

Like some plastics, molded fiberglass convincingly masquerades as other materials, such as terra-cotta, stone, and lead, but it weighs much less. Fiberglass pots hold up very well to the elements and do not chip or readily bend, though a sharp blow will crack them, particularly around the rim. Fiberglass is not cheap; think of it as a very satisfactory midpriced option with both light weight and good looks.

POT TYPES

Let's consider for a few moments the pros and cons of some of the most commonly encountered pot styles.

Rose and Long Tom

Rose pots (featuring an unusually tall, pronounced rim) and long toms (with little or no rim) are both much taller than they are wide. The high soil columns they contain provide excellent drainage, and their dramatic upward lines beautifully complement arching, trailing, and downward-hanging plants. A grouping of several different pot heights with mixed or matched plants can bring to mind a wall of organ pipes or a basalt outcrop.

However, tall pots can be extremely top-heavy and may fall over with the slightest push from the wind or a bump from a fast-moving child or large dog. In fact, sometimes a tall pot topples at the very moment when its contents have grown tall and/or wide enough to overcome the pot's center of gravity, so over it goes. To counteract this poten-

⑩ Vividly-hued ceramics are stunners in the garden, but be sure to choose plants that can stand up to the color competition.

tial problem, fill the base of the pot with a heavy ballast material (such as gravel, stones, or broken bricks), place it within a sturdy metal ring support, or group several tall pots together within a ring of shorter ones. Also be very aware when considering combining a tall plant support (such as a wooden trellis or wrought-iron conical frame) with a tall pot. You might be fighting the most basic forces of nature from the very start.

Standard

If you get out your tape measure or ruler, you will discover that these are about as tall as they are wide, even though they look taller than wide. Like long toms and rose pots, they have a rather high soil column to provide good drainage, and they accentuate plants with linear qualities as well as those with rounded and expansive forms. And they are easy to find in most gardening outlets.

However, like their taller counterparts, they topple over easily when

out of balance with their contents. The remedies for long toms and rose pots will also work with standard pots. Also, I believe the appearance of standard pots borders on the mundane and often fails to complement the plants in them, but you may think otherwise. Allowing plants to spill over their rims can greatly improve the appearance of a standard pot, so by all means use them.

Azalea

Just a little less tall than they are wide, azalea pots appear and are in fact more stable than taller pots. Their low profile allows mounded and spreading plants to look their best in them, and even more-upright plants can interact nicely with them, provided the plants are not too tall. A low center of gravity provides great stability under outside forces; in fact, it takes considerable effort to knock over an azalea pot in physical balance with its contents.

However, plants requiring extremely good drainage may suffer a bit in the relatively short soil column, and some taprooted plants may not be

11 Whether resulting from serendipity or intentional placement, a birdhouse, a few trailing stems of *Clematis montana,* and a well-used glazed pot present a serene tableau.

completely happy in them. Also, a plant much taller than an azalea pot will look ridiculous and fall over readily.

Pan

Also known as bulb pans, these are about half as tall as they are wide and as a result offer great stability (you cannot knock them over, even if you try). Very low-growing plants look great in them—little bulbs such as crocuses and irises, many low-statured succulents, and restrained trailers and spreaders will be displayed to their best advantage in a pan.

The very shallow soil column will present a challenge to any plant requiring very good drainage, so choose the plants for pans carefully. A very fast-draining mix (such as Barad mix, described on page 193) usually overcomes the drainage issue for all but the most fastidious of occupants. Of course, pans are even less suitable for taprooted and tall plants than azalea pots, so avoid using them for such plants.

Hanging Containers

Hanging baskets and similar containers designed to be suspended display trailers, untrained climbers, sprawlers, and arching plants to best effect. Choose from classic wire, utilitarian plastic, lightweight compressed fiber, and even terra-cotta and metal circular baskets, half baskets, mangers, and window boxes.

Like ground-dwelling containers, their shapes interact positively or negatively with plant forms; a tall, bolt-upright plant may look highly self-conscious in a hanging or suspended container. Also, a hanging container's increased surface area and usually greater exposure to wind causes it to dry out more quickly than earthbound containers, so you will need to keep a closer eye on it. The biggest offender is a sphagnum-lined basket, which wicks away soil moisture seemingly as fast as an exhaust fan.

Strawberry Jars

Usually rounded in outline and including several planting pockets distributed regularly around its surface, a strawberry jar makes an excellent choice for a collection of trailing, arching, and spreading plants or a mass of the same kind of plant. A well-planted and filled-in strawberry jar makes its own special statement of abundance and luxuriance.

However, strawberry jars often look gawky and sparse until they fill in, but that problem can be overcome by matching an attractively glazed pot with complementary plants. Combine chartreuse-leaved *Lysimachia nummularia* 'Aurea' with a shiny blue-green strawberry jar to see for yourself how eye-catching a thinly filled-in strawberry jar can be.

Also, a strawberry jar presents a bit of a planting challenge, but following the advice on page 147 will ease the job.

plant groups for containers

THIS BOOK INTENTIONALLY provides no specific directions for combining one particular plant with others in prescribed arrangements. While such "recipes" can offer time-tested combinations or even exciting new partnerships, I believe that you have plenty to draw on while creating wonderful and unique self-made container plantings:

- Your own gardening experience
- Insights and inspiration provided by this book's text and photographs
- Ideas provided by other gardeners' efforts
- Your own personal needs, desires, and sense of taste and design

Many gardeners have asked themselves or other gardeners the question, "Will this grow in a pot?" When asked this question, my initial reply is usually, "Why not give it a try?" Another common question is, "Will these look good together?" To that I reply, "Does it look good to you?" and "Will the container planting look good where you intend to place it?"

You have probably taken the plunge to try out new foods, clothes, decorating styles, sports and games, exercise programs, child-rearing techniques, and forms of entertainment. I heartily recommend that you take the same approach to gardening (in general) and container gardening (in particular). You will discover a big new world out there for you to explore. You won't know if something will grow for you in a pot or if it looks good with another plant until you try it for yourself. So get out there and do it!

❶ The design attributes of two or more plants can interact in bold and powerful ways, such as this lush combination of dark 'Black Parrot' tulips and bronze cordyline foliage.

plant groups for containers | 165

12: annuals

We could get involved in a detailed presentation on the botanical and horticultural meanings of the terms "annual" and "tender" here, but that is really not necessary. For our purposes as container gardeners, an "annual" refers to a plant, often but not always an herbaceous one, that is enjoyed for one season and then discarded or allowed to die at the end of that season. "Tender" indicates a plant that cannot survive frost and cold. So while people in Michigan and Maine enjoy their tender heliotropes and coleus (both shrubs in their native lands) as annuals until frost, others in Southern California and Florida may keep them outdoors year-round as shrubs. Some plants, such as zinnias and sunflowers, are annuals everywhere because they irresistibly follow their genetic programming and complete their entire natural life span—from seed to plant to flower and then again to seed—within a single growing season.

So why bother with plants that normally survive for only one growing season? Annual enthusiasts will

give you plenty of reasons:

- Most grow quickly and often have a long season of interest provided by flowers, foliage, or both (and sometimes even fruit).
- Many offer a great deal of color, which is their primary attribute as a group.
- They are often relatively inexpensive compared to perennials or woody plants.
- New selections offered every year by nurseries satisfy a desire to try the unknown.

Yet another compelling reason to try annuals lies in their expendability; if an annual fails miserably one year, the financial setback is not as substantial as for a disappointing perennial or woody plant. Container gardeners in particular should appreciate the potential for experimentation an annual provides: try a given plant by itself, or in combination with others in a pot, for a season; if it pleases you, repeat your success next year, or try something else if it does not.

A practical reason for exploiting the virtues of annuals stems from their short lives: many grow quite well in cheaper, predominantly peat-based potting mixes, which usually remain in good condition for no more than six months. By the time the mix breaks down, the plants growing in it are dead or nearly so. Longer-lived container plants require more substantial—and generally costlier—potting mixes to support satisfactory growth, such as those

① A cascade of annual *Tagetes* 'Tangerine Gem' creates a delicate curtain of colorful little flowers and sharply scented, finely cut leaves.

② The late-blooming flower clusters of *Leonotis leonurus* bring whimsy and warmth to larger container plantings.

containing bark, coir, or garden soil.

Yes, annuals require yearly replacement (whether by buying anew or by overwintering and repropagating favorites). But since many gardeners approach container plantings as seasonally renewed ventures, the short lives of annuals are not an important issue, especially for anyone who relishes the opportunity to regularly try new plants and combinations.

A few specific points to keep in mind about annuals:

Annuals are easy, but . . . Annuals are often univer-

sally promoted as "easy." Some do in fact require far less care than perennials and shrubs, but as with any plant you need to know and provide the conditions an annual requires for it to thrive (or at least grow). For example, the lean diet that produces an abundant display of blooms from a nasturtium will result in a flower-poor verbena, and the dry soil favored by an arctotis can kill a coleus. People in hot-summer areas lament their inability to enjoy most diascias and nemesias for more than a few weeks, while gardeners in regions with cool summers struggle with amaranthus and castor beans.

Remember the benefits of delayed gratification. Although it is tempting to let an angelonia or a petunia bloom soon after you have potted it, you will enjoy many more blooms after a relatively short waiting period if you pinch the plants once or twice before letting them go into flower-

3 Somber *Capsicum* foliage and richly-colored petunia flowers provide long-lasting companionship for the red cabbage.

4 A close look at *Setaria palmifolia* 'Rubra' reveals its strong linear quality and fine surface texture, almost subliminal when viewing the whole coarse plant.

production mode. Heliotropes, pentas, and leonotis also produce far more colorful flower displays if pinched a few times, and a great many foliage annuals, including perillas, basils, iresines, pelargoniums, and coleus, fill out and look far more impressive after a few pinchings as well. On the other hand, some annuals, such as ornamental peppers, impatiens, mimulus, scarlet sage, and verbenas, do not require pinching to make a completely satisfying plant.

A SELECTION OF ANNUALS FOR CONTAINERS

- **Alternanthera ficoidea**—This fine-textured, low-growing, shaggy foliage plant is available in many vibrant or rich colors, often with two or three on a given plant. Excellent for contrasting with or echoing the colors of its companions. Pinch (or shear) to encourage bushy, compact growth. Thrives in heat.

- **Angelonia**—Small, elegant, orchidlike flowers appear for months in combinations of white, purple, and dusty pink on linear, graceful spikes above fine foliage. Pinch young plants a couple of times for more flowers, though a many-stemmed plant might fall over unless supported.

- **Capsicum annuum**—Ornamental peppers provide a lot of south-of-the-border colors and various textures with their fruit and foliage, especially variegated ones such as 'Jigsaw'. Many excellent ones are available, including 'Ignite', 'Explosive Ember', 'Chilly Chili', 'Super Chili', 'Medusa', 'Salsa Yellow', 'Favorite Yellow', 'Blast', 'Masquerade', and 'Thai Hot'. 'Black Pearl' and others with near-black foliage combine memorably with pink, chartreuse, pale yellow, orange, red, and even magenta foli-

age and flowers. Stunning when multiple plants of the same cultivar are in one pot. Larger-growing selections are sometimes worth trying to overwinter for a second season. Very heat tolerant and revives quickly if watered when wilted.

- **Centaurea and Senecio**—Dusty millers provide quietly gorgeous gray to nearly silver foliage that looks good with almost anything. Some are finely cut; others look much coarser. Cut off elongating spikes that usu-

⑤ *Diascias* (twinspurs) is being bred to withstand more heat, offering fine texture and warm flower colors to a larger gardening audience.

⑥ Like the *Setaria* noted here (page 174), *Pennisetum setaceum* 'Purpureum' is perennial in warmer areas but attains a good size and attractive habit when grown as a single-season annual.

⑥

ally produce dirty yellow flowers. Drought tolerant.

- **Diascia**—Loose, often gently trailing, fine-textured mounds bear candy-colored blooms (look for the pink and apricot shades). Most prefer cooler weather, but more heat-tolerant selections are being released.

- **Heliotropium arborescens**—On most top-ten lists solely because of the relaxing vanilla or baby-powder fragrance of their flowers, heliotropes also provide good-sized masses of white and shades of purple that attract butterflies. Pinch young plants a few times and deadhead regularly. These shrubby plants are worth trying to overwinter for a second season and make sensuous topiaries.

- **Hemigraphis 'Exotica'**—Waffle-textured, near-black foliage literally shines in bright sun and provides a superb background for strong and pastel colors. Low growing and well behaved. Remove the little off-white flowers if they bother you.

- **Impatiens**—Common as dirt but just as useful, especially those with

variegated foliage (white-marked ones for shade and colorful New Guinea selections for sunnier spots). Nurseries offer many bright and pastel flower colors to choose from. Show your gardening friends how interesting these plants can be by combining them with bold textures and other colors.

- **Iresine herbstii**—Shrubby plants in, well, loud colors (nuclear yellow, lurid magenta, bloody red), these should be pinched a few times and then let go as part of explosive color combinations. Overwinter a few for larger, even more assertive plants the following season.

- **Leonotis leonurus**—One of the few annuals that blooms very late in the season, with whorls (clusters) of uncompromisingly bright orange, tubular flowers at the top of tall, leafy stems. Use as a pleasant green filler in a container for most of the season, and then stand

⑦ A shy producer of flowers (unlike many of its ivy geranium relatives), the gold-netted foliage of *Pelargonium peltatum* 'The Crocodile' provides a bit of color and fine texture to coarser, more boldly colored companions (here, *Tibouchina urvilleana*).

back and wait for the questions and compliments. Pinch a couple of times for bushier plants and give ample water and fertilizer.

- **Leucanthemum (Melampodium) paludosum**—Small golden daisies decorate neat, sturdy, steadily expanding "bushes" over the entire season. Use singularly, in a group planting, or with taller or cascading plants. A workhorse, not a diva.

- **Ocimum basilicum**—Yes, this is culinary basil, and most selections are equally pleasing in the garden or on the tongue. Use green-leaved types for their full, abundant form, and dark ones as a foil for many other colors—as you would dark-leaved selections of *Capsicum, Hemigraphis,* or *Solenostemon* (*Coleus*). Don't forget to smell it as you pass by or to cut some on your way to the kitchen.

- **Osteospermum**—Happy daisies appear above coarse mounds of gray-green foliage. Choose from white, blue, and lavender shades as well as yellow, and do your best to figure out how to include the fantastical 'Whirligig' and similar selections with spoon-shaped "petals." Most prefer cooler weather, but progress is being made on selections that take more heat.

- **Pelargonium**—Geraniums, as they are commonly called, have it all: colorful flowers and foliage, spiky lines (their bloom stalks), solid form (if pinched occasionally), a lot of space (between the flowers and the foliage), and textures ranging from impossibly fine to stolidly coarse. Some are prized for their fragrance (in lemon and other fruity scents as well as mint, pine, and sharper essences), although some noses dislike the strong aromas of many of the larger-growing zonal selections. Two of the very best of the smaller growers are 'Bird Dancer' (dense yet delicate spiky foliage marked with dark red-brown) and 'Vancouver Centennial' (gold and burgundy toothed foliage and orange-red flowers—wow!). Many do better in cooler weather and out of strong sun.

- **Pentas lanceolata**—Decidedly happy-looking plants bear clusters of starry flowers in white, red, pink, and lavender. Unpinched plants usually bloom sparsely and therefore deprive butterflies and hummingbirds of what would otherwise be a feast on mounded, very long-blooming plants.

- **Perilla 'Magilla'**—Coleus-like 'Magilla' offers creative designers a foliage palette of dark purple-red, medium green, white, and magenta borne on sturdy plants. Use one unpinched plant in a combination pot for a frisson of contrasting color, or feature a big, pinched plant in a pot by itself. The truly adventuresome allow the violet-blue flower spikes to add to the fun.

- **Salvia coccinea**—Less assertive than its common cousin (*Salvia splendens,* scarlet sage), Texas sage offers open, airy spikes of white, pink, coral, and red flowers over most of the season. A pinch or two delays bloom, and it is worth the wait. Use to open up the look of dense plantings and to attract butterflies and hummingbirds.

- **Setaria palmifolia 'Rubra'**—This perennial grass looks its best when grown for one lusty season: give it plenty of water and fertilizer to produce an open, arching mass of cornlike, red-toned stems bearing long, deeply ribbed, medium to dark green leaves. Grow several plants in a large pot as a focal point or include one for contrast in a combination pot.

- **Solenostemon scutellarioides**—Do you still think all coleus are dumpy and garish? Check out the thousand or so selections now available for a revealing look at this number-one annual for foliage color. There is a color, plant habit (spreading, upright, or trailing), or degree of sun tolerance to combine with virtually every container plant. Trust me.

- **Tagetes**—All of the shorter, flower-dense marigolds do well in well-drained containers, but look for the 'Gem' series in shades of yellow and orange. Their smaller, less abundant flowers and fine foliage add a delicate touch. People love or hate the scent of the foliage.

- **Tropaeolum majus**—Like marigolds, nasturtiums benefit from conditions that many gardeners would consider less than optimal. For the best bloom, take it easy on the nitrogen, don't water heavily, and provide plenty of sun. Long-stalked, rounded, light- to medium-green leaves (sometimes darker with moody red tones) provide an uncommon shape and medium to coarse tex-

Many violas and pansies can provide color for several months, far longer than most warm- and hot-season annuals, so don't pass them over.

ture. Don't forget to eat the flowers, which come in hot colors as well as a few less fiery ones.

- **Verbena bonariensis**—An upright verbena instead of a trailer (see page 201 for a description of climbers versus trailers), this member of the genus provides feelings of line and space in no uncertain terms. Often used as a see-through screen in borders, it can play a similar role in a pot. The purple flowers attract butterflies, which will make the plants bob and dance in response to their actions.

- **Viola**—You want color? Think violas and their larger-flowered kin, pansies. They come in a vast color range and bloom prolifically and steadily on low-grow-ing to mounded, sometimes loosely spreading plants. Although generally cool-season workhorses, some are more heat tolerant.

13: aquatics

Who can deny the basic, mysterious, and sensual nature of water? We drink it, cook with it, bathe in it, play in it, pay good money to have houses near it or vacation by it, and of course garden with it. It provides fascinating reflections, appealing pictures in motion, soothing sounds, and a habitat for a diverse range of life-forms. But water gardening is only for people with enough space for a pond, and a pond takes up a good deal of space and time, right? The answer to that is an emphatic and very encouraging "No!" If you can grow a plant in a mix-filled pot somewhere in your garden, you can also enjoy aquatic plants in containers. Just make sure to use pots without drainage holes.

That last statement is not entirely correct, actually. Many of the plants considered aquatic—including quite a few of the ones in this chapter's plant list—do well in very moist soil in a drained pot. If you do not own any undrained pots or simply choose not

① A container provides an ideal watery habitat for a miniature water lily (*Nymphaea* 'Helvola') floating among its earth-anchored companions.

to acquire any, and you wish to grow some of these plants, be prepared to water your containers frequently (especially in summer), or put a couple of pieces of fine-mesh screening over the drainage holes. Water will still flow out, just quite slowly. Also, use a potting mix that contains plenty of organic matter and real garden soil if possible, avoiding fast-draining mixes containing large amounts of porous mineral materials such as perlite or pumice.

If you do choose to garden in undrained containers, many pleasures await, provided you keep a few important points in mind:

Location and size. Assuming a container holds water (it has no hole, or the hole has been completely plugged with a resin or epoxy sealant, and there are no cracks to let water seep out), only its size and position in the garden pose any significant limitations. Just make sure that the location can support the weight of a planted aquatic container; it will weigh more than the same container filled with potting mix. Some decks, balconies, and roofs might strain under the weight.

Adding fish. If you play host to fish and other creatures, you will need to feed them and make sure the water chemistry suits their needs.

Mosquitos. The more water you manage, the greater the need to watch out for a population explosion of mosquito wigglers.

Bad odors. Aquatic gardening sometimes brings unpleasant odors with it, particularly at season's end, when you will need to drain the water from the containers. The accumulated leaves and other decomposing organic debris at the bottom can smell nasty, but the odor does not last long once the materials are exposed to the air.

Keeping things in the pot. Finally, if your aquatic plants grow in their own individual pots within a larger water-holding container (quite often the case), surround the pot and potting-mix surface with burlap or screening, or place heavy gravel or pebbles on the surface, to prevent the mix—and any perlite or other floatable constituent—from rising out of the pot and cluttering the surface of the water.

Beyond the usual horticultural satisfaction of growing attractive plants in containers, aquatic gardening provides unique opportunities for creative designers. A container holding only water creates a natural mirror that reflects other parts of the garden, the sky, or the admirer. Adding a solitary plant or a number of them to that watery context increases the reflections and doubles the apparent participants in a garden scene. If you do not care about reflections, you can grow a "groundcover" of a floating plant, such as *Azolla* or *Salvinia*. You might even choose to grow floaters exclusively in a container to produce a low-maintenance, high-interest object with a living, and sometimes moving, surface.

A SELECTION OF AQUATICS FOR CONTAINERS

- **Acorus gramineus**—All grassy-leaved sweet flags offer an abundance of line and textural interest, and some selections offer attractive variegated or golden foliage as a bonus. My favorite is 'Nana Aurea', a diminutive, golden, almost threadleaf form barely four inches tall. It is cute (a word I rarely use, but perfect here) as a single specimen in small containers and eye-catching as an accent or even a groundcover in larger combination plantings.

- **Azolla**—If you are feeling playful, float a few mosquito ferns in an undrained, glazed bowl that holds at least a few inches of water, and then watch as the plants seem to grow before your eyes. The red and green coloration and intricate patterns of *A. caroliniana* and *A. filiculoides* will grab anyone's attention. If they grow so thickly that you cannot appreciate their form anymore, remove some of them and let them readjust themselves. Or not: a thick mass of them makes a conversation piece too.

- **Carex**—See page 214 for a detailed description of these plants, many of which enjoy an aquatic lifestyle.

- **Cyperus**—All papyrus evokes images of ancient Egyptian depictions of the Nile. Whether tall (*C. papyrus*), medium (*C. involucratus*), or shorter (*C. profiler*), these plants offer irresistible line interest and fine texture. Don't be surprised when garden visitors cannot resist the urge to stroke these plants or pretend to use them as parasols.

- **Eichhornia crassipes**—Decidedly different, water hyacinths offer a fascinating rounded form and an ethereal flower color (blue-pink-lavender, to my eyes, with yellow-orange markings). They float and sail on the water's surface unless they grow so thickly that they jostle each other out. A terrible waterway weed where they are hardy and a design statement wherever they are used in moderation.

- **Eleocharis montevidensis**—If you want to add extremely fine texture and plenty of line interest, use a few plants of fiber-optic grass in specimen pots or in combinations. Their fresh green foliage provides even more eye appeal. A shake of the pot will help improve the appearance of a messy "hairdo," as will a gentle "combing" with widely spaced fingers.

- **Equisetum**—You want to incorporate distinctive lines in an aquatic planting? Horsetails are without question one of your go-to plants. They are almost nothing but line and space, with some green and brown added to

2 A decidedly healthy *Azolla* seems to be marching out of its red-glazed, water-filled container. Near-abstractions such as this can bring another level of fascination and sophistication to a garden.

ornament them. As you might expect from something that predates many dinosaurs, horsetails are very tough and adaptable.

- **Houttuynia cordata 'Chameleon'**—A thug in the open ground, engulfing almost anything in its path, this plant behaves much better when contained in a pot. The green leaves edged in red and cream combine with many other colors, and their orange-peel fragrance sur-

prises anyone who rubs them. White flowers appear erratically.

- **Hydrocotyle**—Pennyworts *(H. umbellata* and *H. verticillata)* offer intriguing round, Tropaeolum-like leaves held well above the potting mix (or water) on thin stems, bringing form and space interest to any planting that can accommodate their exuberant growth. Cut overzealous plants back to the ground, and they will

③

soon spring back. Tiny greenish white flowers add a breath of contrast to the highly defined foliage.

- **Juncus effusus 'Spiralis'**—One word: line. Young plants look like green scribbles, and an older plant suggests madness. They arch, they twist, they look like they want to jump out of the pot, and in the process they produce a specimen or contrast plant par excellence. Keep scissors handy to trim off the brown leaf tips if they bother you.

- **Ludwigia sedioides**—Once seen and never forgotten, the mosaic plant recalls Moorish tile patterns or computer-generated designs. Grow this prima donna by itself in a wide, low bowl and then marvel at how the plant routinely contracts at night and then expands during the day.

- **Marsilea**—Well described by its common name, water clover (actually ferns) rises out of the water or floats like four-part crystal patterns on the surface. Divide marsilea when their abundance obscures the individual form of the leaves.

- **Myriophyllum**—Called "milfoils" in many reference books, but I propose to call them "water feathers." Whether submerged or emerging from the water, few plants offer as fine a texture, and their gently curving lines add interest as well. You will need to thin them occasionally to prevent congestion.

- **Nelumbo nucifera**—If papyrus reminds us of the Nile, then lotuses transport us to India and China. Giant round leaves hover over the water on long stalks, and water-lily-like blooms, mostly in pink and white, capture and hold the eye. Showerhead seedpods add a third distinctive form. See what happens when you allow water to drop from your hand onto the leaves: I dare you to resist playing with lotuses after that.

- **Nymphaea**—Certainly the sine qua non of many inground water gardens, water lilies can play a part

❸ Pitcher plants thrive in undrained containers filled with consistently moist, long-fibered sphagnum moss.

❹ An overhead view reveals the layered patterns formed by a burgeoning colony of *Pistia stratiotes,* or water lettuce—a perfect example of the power of simplicity.

in container gardening, especially *N. tetragona* 'Helvola', which lives happily in a whiskey barrel or similar container. Grow smaller water lilies as solo specimens or as the stars in larger containers.

- **Oryza sativa 'Nigrescens'**—Black rice, like other dark-leaved plants, offers a foil for many other foliage colors, but this plant provides its own contrasting red and green highlights among the upright-arching leaves. Pale flowers and fruits—yes, actual rice—create more interest. Easy to grow from seed if birds, mice, and other creatures do not gobble it up first.

- **Pistia stratiotes**—If you do not want to actually grow this plant but you would like the look of it for a few hours, simply place some small heads of loose leaf lettuce on the surface of the water and hope they float. Or start with a few plants at the beginning of the season and have a lot of them by season's end. Feature a few plants by themselves on the water's sur-

face, cover the surface with them, or use them in combination pots: you will love the look.

- **Pontederia cordata**—Pickerel-weed catches your eye with its bright blue flower stalks born all summer against a backdrop of elongated heart-shaped leaves. Dragonflies perching on the flowers between their mad dashes further animate an aquatic planting. Thin the leaves occasionally to retain the interesting spaces between them.

- **Sagittaria latifolia**—The triangular white flowers certainly attract attention during their rather brief blooming season, but it is those arrowhead leaves that create an unmistakable season-long presence of form. As for many plants with strong leaf forms, you might want to thin the leaves every now and then to draw attention to each leaf.

- **Salvinia**—Another genus of floating fern (like *Azolla*), *Salvinia* grows rapidly and is best managed for optimum results. Much coarser-looking than *Azolla*, it brings a fresher green color and the suggestion of fat caterpillars

lolling on the water. If that does not sound creepy to you, give *Salvinia* a try.

- **Sarracenia**—Who can resist the visual and natural appeal of a plant that looks like agitated cobras and digests the victims that fall into its traps? Spaceshiplike flowers add to the allure. Pitcher plants (and their relatives in the genus *Darlingtonia*) look like nothing else in the plant kingdom and instantly give their owners an air of horticultural panache.

- **Typha minima**—While big cattail species certainly command attention, they are too large and vigorous for anything other than a very large container (or pond, for that matter). This dwarf cattail, on the other hand, brings the linear attraction of its big relatives to a container, but on a much more manageable and far more delicate scale. Diminutive brown flower spikes—the cattails—reinforce the demure appearance.

⑤ Papyrus of any height—they vary from one- to eight-feet-tall—can elicit all sorts of visual associations with their airy attitude.

14: bulbs

For our purposes, the term "bulb" includes not only true bulbs such as tulips and lilies, but also corms (crocuses, for example), tubers and tuberous roots (dahlias and gloriosa lilies), and rhizomes (cannas and irises). All of these forms enable plants to survive during times of stress or less-than-optimal conditions, and for gardeners they provide convenient "packages" for easy handling, storage, and transportation. Just think of how much simpler it is to store and plant a bag of tulip bulbs than it is to maintain an equal number of actively growing geraniums, and you will understand why bulbs find favor among many gardeners. Of course, their vast range of colors as a group makes them mighty appealing as well. Only annuals (as a group) provide as much opportunity to play with color.

Keep in mind that hardy bulbs (those that will survive winter outdoors with little or no protection) must be grown and maintained differently from nonhardy bulbs (those that perish if left outdoors in winter). Whether you endure a harsh Wisconsin winter or a much more benign one in Arizona, hardy bulbs need to experience some measure of cold to bloom well, and nonhardy bulbs require protection from damaging low temperatures and other challenging factors in order to simply survive.

Many bulbs have an active growth period during which they bloom and/or produce attractive foliage. Sooner or later hardy bulbs heed an internal call to prepare for harder times ahead (usually a hot, dry summer followed by winter), while nonhardy bulbs often get struck down in their prime by frost. In either case, container gardeners need to be aware of these downtimes and should be prepared to deal with them.

After you have enjoyed tulips or daffodils or other hardy bulbs in containers, the easiest way to cope with their unsightly yellowing foliage is simply to discard the plants. Many container-grown hardy bulbs provide one grand display, and that's that. Just as you can bring a poinset-

❶ A bag of hyacinth bulbs holds the promise of masses of bright, clear colors and one-of-a-kind fragrance for the following spring.

tia into flower a second time by following a detailed and precise growing regimen, you might be able to do the same for many hardy bulbs. However, the results are unpredictable at best, so it is tempting to discard the bulbs and start again next autumn with new ones.

Nonhardy bulbs present a mixed bag of attributes and cultural needs: Some, such as calla lilies and pineapple lilies, bloom briefly (but often spectacularly) and require specialized care to bring them into bloom again; whether you choose to provide that care is up to you. Others bloom for a long time (such as tuberous begonias) or remain attractive in leaf as long as they are in active growth (such as caladiums and the *Alocasia/Colocasia/Xanthosoma* complex). If you do a little research, you will discover a big world of container-worthy bulbs to explore.

So yes, you can grow tulips and dahlias in pots. Give

2 Assertive *Colchicum* makes its appearance in fall, when most other hardy bulbs are long past their time in the sun.

3 *Iris bucharica* flowers appear for a short time in spring, but their straplike foliage persists much longer and has a strong linear presence in pots.

them the same basic care that you would give them in the open ground, but keep in mind that they will need a little more watering and fertilizing in their container home.

A SELECTION OF HARDY BULBS FOR CONTAINERS

- **Colchicum**—Here is a twist on your normal bulb: Many colchicums bloom in fall, after sending up leaves in spring that then die down for the summer. Most bloom in loud and proud variations of magenta, but some offer less strident violet or white flowers. It is probably best to pot them while dormant in late summer, enjoy the blooms, and then plant them out in the garden before the ground freezes.
- **Crocus**—Harbingers of spring for many people, crocuses force well in (preferably rather shallow) pots to produce cheerful spots of color early in the container-gardening season. Stagger the removal times from cold storage to prolong their season of interest. Don't skimp on the number you put into a pot; placing them cheek by jowl will

produce the showiest display. Start with selections of *C. chrysanthus* and the Dutch hybrids, then move on to other species and their selections.

- **Hyacinthus**—Beloved for their fragrance, hyacinths force easily, but don't use the giant exhibition-sized bulbs for general garden use. Smaller bulbs produce smaller, more graceful bloom spikes less likely to clumsily bend or collapse under their own weight. Of course you can stake the big boys, but they often look like they belong in a pot at a flower show instead of outside in a garden.

- **Iris**—The gnomelike and fragrant selections of *I. reticulata* and its relatives can be grown and displayed much like crocuses and other smaller ("minor") bulbs. Try the much taller, miniature-corn-like *I. bucharica* in roomy pots; the plants grow from clusters of brittle, thickened roots, so be careful when potting them. Forget trying to grow the more familiar bearded and beardless irises in pots. While they may survive, they rarely put on much of a display compared to those in the open ground.

- **Lilium**—Lilies require a much longer active growth period than the rest of the bulbs here, but the results are worth it: the colors and fragrances available are varied and sumptuous, even voluptuous. Unlike most hardy bulbs, lilies may increase in strength after a year or two in a roomy pot, provided they are watered and fertilized well during growth. Use a pot of lilies as a focal point or line up a few pots to make a temporary low wall.

- **Muscari**—Grape hyacinths bloom later and are a bit more work than many other hardy bulbs, but their mostly intense blues and virginal whites make an impressive display. Their grapelike flower clusters provide an interesting change of shape compared with most hardy bulbs, and the grassy foliage adds some linear appeal. As for many of the smaller hardy bulbs, pack them in the pot for the greatest color impact.

- **Narcissus**—Daffodils are without question my favorite bulb to force, because they give plenty of bang for the buck, many require rather short forcing periods, and they seem to shout "Spring!" Little pots of the miniature kinds make extremely portable spots of color, and larger pots of the bigger sorts automatically become focal points. If cost is an issue (and it might well be; good-quality bulbs are not cheap), don't pack the pot tightly with bulbs; even a few daffodils in a pot get the point across.

- **Scilla**—While the flower colors closely resemble those found in grape hyacinths, scillas produce squat spikes of starry flowers, giving them a finer visual texture. Like crocuses and other little bulbs, they look best in bulb pans or azalea pots, preferably not in new, raw-looking terra-cotta.

- **Tulipa**—Who doesn't love tulips? They have the widest color range of any spring-blooming hardy bulb, their flowers range from simple goblets to elegant lily-like blooms to peonylike doubles, and their blue-green foliage goes well with many colors, including raw terra-cotta. Even orange and pink tulips do not clash with their terra-cotta pots, thanks to the visual mediation of the intervening foliage. Among all of the hundreds of available tulips, named selections of midseason-blooming tulips usually do best in pots; try them first before attempting late-blooming kinds or many of the species.

A SELECTION OF NONHARDY BULBS FOR CONTAINERS

- **Alocasia/Colocasia/Xanthosoma complex**—This group provides all five design elements in spades: many shades of green and yellow, plus white and near black; exuberant upward and arching line; sculptural form; plenty of readily perceptible space contained within their big leaves; and undeniably bold texture. Many are genetically predisposed to supersized dimensions (hence the general common name, elephant's ears), so fertilize and water them amply for the most stupefying results.

- **Begonia**—I am not big on the tuberous ones, simply because I have never been able to grow them in the hot, humid summers of the East and Midwest. However, readers in gentler climates should not deprive them-

④ An iron cross clover (*Oxalis deppei*), shown here with an annual lobelia, can be stored dormant in a pot with no water, then brought out in spring to start up again. For best results, divide and repot every other year.

selves of their sumptuous multiple petticoats in many hot colors as well as pink and white (see Chapter 18, Tropicals, for other begonias that almost everyone should try).

- **Caladium**—Think of these as smaller elephant's ears but in much fancier dress; many sport flashy combinations of green, white, red, and pink. The predominantly pink and red ones look miserable in a raw terra-cotta pot, so think about growing them in gray or brown or darker terra-cotta pots. The green and white selections look splendid in shiny-glazed pots, especially black, dark blue, or oxblood ones.

- **Canna**—Don't think of cannas exclusively as producers of colorful flowers in hot colors: even the ones with plain green leaves have an imposing presence in a pot, to say nothing of the strikingly variegated ones. Give them plenty of room and combine them with less bold-looking partners, such as grasses or *Salvia coccinea*.

⑤ Calla lilies combine sumptuous foliage with strongly suggestive flowers. This pot of *Zantedeschia* 'Deep Throat' appears to be in constant motion.

⑥ *Eucomis zambesiaca* (pineapple lily) blooms rather quickly after planting, but the flower spikes can last a month or more.

- **Dahlia**—Dahlias in pots? Absolutely, but usually not the monster-sized ones; they would look a little self-conscious in anything other than a very large container. Many smaller growers, especially selections with single flowers, make fine container subjects. Take advantage of their wide range of flower color, spacious growth habit, and rather coarse texture, and by all means consider the ones with dark foliage, such as 'Bishop of Llandaff' and its kin.

- **Eucomis**—Unlike any other bulb in appearance, a pineapple lily is well described by its common name. From the center of a lush rosette of strappy leaves arises a thick stem bearing a dense spike of starry flowers topped with a crown of leaflike bracts. Many offer green foliage and white flowers, but 'Sparkling Burgundy' stands out with dark red-toned leaves and pinkish flowers. Enjoy the flower spike while it lasts, but the foliage looks good almost all season.

- **Gloriosa superba**—Basically a climbing lily: the leaf tips bear threadlike tendrils, by which the plant scrambles up another smallish plant or trellis. The flashy orange and red flowers look like little campfires or tiny tropical birds in full mating plumage. Flowering is brief but unforgettable.

- **Oxalis**—These mostly small plants offer a wide range of shamrock foliage and cheerful flowers. Mounded to lax, plain green to dark purple foliage, often attractively marked with a contrasting color, serves as a foil to white, pink, yellow, or purple flowers. Great plants for providing midrange texture. Like their weedy cousins, the leaves close up at night.

- **Zantedeschia**—Calla lilies may be brief flowering, but their lush foliage, sometimes splashed with silver or toned with dark red, adds linear and textural interest all season. Get over the stereotype that insists the flowers are funereal; their pure colors and elegantly sculptural form are worthy of the choicest pot.

- **Zephyranthes**—The grassy leaves of rain lilies provide linear interest for most of the season, then demure, lily-like blooms in white, pink, or yellow magically appear after a rain shower or a good watering. I think they look their best in simple, low containers displayed on a plinth or at the edge of a flight of steps.

15: cacti and other succulents

If many bulbs and their ilk are valued principally for their color, then cacti and other succulents are the plants to turn to for form. Yes, many dazzle us with their silky, almost psychedelic flowers, and they do offer the entire range of textures and many colors, but those sculptural, bizarre, sometimes animal-like shapes are what offer seemingly limitless opportunities for creative compositions. If one of them in a pot brings to mind an objet d'art, then a collection of them recalls an entire gallery.

A popularly held notion asserts that all cacti and other succulents are easy to grow. This is the same as saying all annuals are grown for their flowers or that dahlias cannot be grown in containers. While many cacti and other succulents survive for years with minimal care, some of them thrive with more attentive care, and a few of them are among the most challenging plants to keep alive in cultivation.

As they do benefit from some specialized care, here are a few points to keep in mind:

Use a porous potting mix. Most cacti and other succulents require a very well-drained mix, high in porous ingredients and relatively low in organic matter. Many cactophiles use a mix (often called Barad mix after its formulator, Dr. Gerald Barad) that combines 50 percent mineral particles with 50 percent organic matter:

- 3 parts commercial potting mix high in bark and/or coir (composted coconut fiber)
- 2 parts pumice (a mineral product similar to, but structurally stronger than, perlite or vermiculite)
- 1 part Turface (this product is similar to cat litter but it doesn't break down)

Such a mix allows water to drain through quickly yet retains enough moisture around the roots to prevent desiccation. Although the high porosity translates to the need for surprisingly frequent watering during active growth, it also means that virtually no water exists in the mix when plants are dormant. This is a good thing. Read on.

Observe the dormant period. Like many other plants, most cacti and other succulents require some down time to ensure continued healthy growth, but their rest does not always occur during winter. While the great majority of cacti are winter dormant, many other succulents want to grow actively in winter, whether in a greenhouse or on a windowsill or outdoors (if hardy). Too much water during dormancy will kill many cacti and other succulents. When it doubt, don't water them. Generally, if a plant loses its luster or begins to shrink during its normal period of active growth, it is definitely time to give it water. However, if you notice shriveling occurring as dormancy approaches, resist the urge to keep watering as much as usual, because the onset of dormancy is a signal to begin to reduce (but not suddenly stop) watering. An infrequent dribble of water—barely enough to slightly moisten the surface of the mix—should keep most dormant cacti and other succulents happy. Dormancy often results in a leafless plant, so don't be surprised if a plant you bought in spring drops all of its leaves in fall. Learn a plant's dormancy needs before adopting it.

❶ A young specimen of *Pachypodium namaquanum* makes an impact in a carefully chosen container. It will soon need to be moved, however, into a larger pot to keep growing without check.

Full sun is not always required. Holiday cacti and some others break the cactus mold by requiring shade at certain times of the year and in regions with naturally strong sunshine. Similarly, many haworthias and a good number of euphorbias must be protected from strong sun to avoid scarred and stunted growth. Again, do a little research before attempting to grow these plants.

Keep them hot year-round? All of these plants grow in deserts, and deserts are always hot, right? Wrong. Many do grow in arid regions of the world, but these areas are not always hot. Deserts can get cold, and many cacti and other succulents can withstand surprisingly low temperatures, often to freezing and sometimes far below. On the other hand, temperatures below 55°F (13°C) will kill many of them. Get out the books, go online, and ask questions.

Know their individual growth rates. While many succulents grow at amazingly slow rates—and sometimes do not appear to grow at all over a given season—others approach weediness in their exuberance. Many sedums and hens and chicks (*Sempervivum*) multiply like bunnies, and a climbing onion (*Bowiea*) can easily produce a five-foot thready stem in one season before going totally dormant. Use that vigor to produce an impressive display in a relatively short time.

Handle with care. Finally, don't be put off by the prickly nature of many of these plants—just be careful when near them or when handling them. Also realize that many succulents are quite fleshy and even brittle and can be damaged by rough handling.

Treat your cacti and other succulents as you would any other plant—by providing for their needs—and you will find them just as rewarding (maybe more so) as a petunia, ivy, or geranium. Look back to Part 1 on the elements of design to see a great many cacti and other succulents used beautifully and creatively.

A SELECTION OF CACTI AND OTHER SUCCULENTS FOR CONTAINERS

- **Aeonium arboreum 'Zwartkop'**— The solitary rosettes of young, unbranched plants provide interesting circular outlines, while older, multistemmed specimens bring to mind colonies of prehistoric underwater creatures. The

rosettes of plants grown in full sun look like shiny black old fashioned roses to me.

- **Agave**—Like aeoniums, agaves offer another useful group of flowerlike rosette forms, and some might even suggest the tentacles of squids, especially larger, older

examples of *A. americana* and its selections. Variegated forms make stunning specimen plants, while a group of several smaller ones in a roomy pot makes an assertive statement of color and form.

- **Aloe**—Most aloes have thick leaves in dense clusters or rosettes and rather coarse textures, especially *A. ferox*. Others, such as *A. vera* (used for treating burns) are more open and reveal a great deal of space between their quite linear leaves.

- **Beaucarnea recurvata**—Remember the exploited truffula trees of Dr. Seuss's tale about the Lorax? Pony-

2 Like many succulents, the dark but reflective rosettes of *Aeonium arboreum* 'Zwartkop' resemble undersea creatures. Their depth of color is related to the amount of sun they receive.

3 *Sempervivum* and the related *Jovivarba* and *Rosularia* grow best in a well-drained medium with plenty of sun, although they tolerate shade if not kept too wet.

tail palms remind me of them, with bushy heads of strappy foliage above bare, sometimes gently curved trunks arising from swollen bases. Use solitary specimens as a focal point or as part of a grouping of containers.

- **Bowiea volubilis**—Basically looking like a mass of green threads coming out of a paper-covered bulb, climbing onion lends fine texture and bright green accents to a composition. Train the stems on a form or over another plant, or let them dangle from a pot or hanging basket.
- **Ceropegia linearis subsp. woodii**—Several rosary vine plants put together create a fine-textured veil of silver-marked foliage dangling from a hanging basket or tall pot, while a single stringy stem offers a bit of contrast to other plants it may clamber over. The little "potatoes" sometimes produced where the leaves join the stem can be used to start new plants.
- **Crassula**—With time, *C. arborescens* and *C. ovata*, the silver jade and regular jade plants, become thick-stemmed, coarse-textured

miniature "trees" that look much older than their age. *C. perfoliata* var. *minor*, perfectly described by its common name, propeller plant, appears to be constantly spinning. All three species mix attractively with linear and rosette shapes.

- **Echeveria**—Resembling in basic form their more cold-tolerant relatives (sempervivums, commonly known as hens and chicks), echeverias offer a wider variety of colors—including icy green, ghostly gray-blue, and moody dark purple—in visually engaging rosettes, many sporting wavy edges. Flowers in hot shades appear on arch-

ing stems above the plants, and the rosettes do not die after flowering, unlike hens and chicks.

- **Epiphyllum crenatum**—Use this plant as a "what is that?" note in a planting. Zigzag stems (no, they are not leaves) grow in unpredictable directions and offer a unique combination of line and form, unforgettably spilling out of a

④ A strawberry jar pocket provides an excellent home for *Sempervivum arachniodeum* (the cobweb houseleek), which quickly fills out. (While appreciating the drainage offered by a jar, these older plants need heavier water.)

⑤ The solid structure of *Agave ferox* perfectly complements soft, airier grasses such as this *Muhlenbergia dumosa*.

large pot or hanging basket. Feel fortunate when the water-lily-like blooms appear.

- **Euphorbia**—Many euphorbias are best left by themselves as showy individual specimens, but *E. lactea* and *E. tirucallii* mix nicely with other succulents in mixed pots. Milkbush *(E. tirucallii)* resembles spiky, lumpy green animal horns, while the stems of *E. lactea* look like handfuls of thin green pencils (lit with red in the selection 'Sticks on Fire').

- **Graptopetalum paraguayense**— The common names ghost plant and mother-of-pearl plant derive evocatively from the very useful, almost pastel coloration (in shades of blue, gray, and pink) of the rosettes of thick leaves. Sensational when combined with anything pink, dark blue or purple, or gray, including pots and topdressings.

- **Hoya**—Wax plants provide plenty of linear interest to a container, especially when dangling from a hanging basket or trained onto a hoop. Clusters of waxy, starry flowers add some color and punctuate the overall linear appearance.

Have patience with these; many grow slowly.

- **Kalanchoe**—Here is a feast of colors, forms, and textures: *K. beharensis* (felt bush) produces roughly triangular, brown-tinged, finely haired leaves on big, coarse plants. *K. pumila* makes a gently cascading, fine-looking mass of small, almost chalky leaves and lilac flowers in late winter. And *K. thyrsiflora* looks like a nested stack of red-edged, greenish-gray, thick-cut potato chips.

- **Opuntia**—While most members of this genus seem to inject their tiny, persistently itchy spines into your skin just by looking at them, don't give up on the entire group: some of the less pernicious or even spineless species (such as *O. ficus-indica* var. *inermis*) make eye-catching, coarse-textured accent plants or focal points.

- **Pachyphytum**—These are basically elongated versions of their *Graptopetalum* relatives (listed above) but are usually more rounded and softer looking. Most, including the chubby, poetically named moonstones (*P. oviferum*), appear to be covered with frost or dusted with confectioner's sugar.

- **Pachypodium**—With age, most pachypodiums become statuesque, treelike specimen plants covered in spines, and they bear explosive-looking leaf rosettes. Grow them by themselves in their own pots or group them with mounded, less coarse-looking plants for a study in contrast of form and texture.

- **Portulacaria afra**—Simply put, the elephant bush looks like a more refined and relaxed jade tree (*Crassula ovata*, listed above). Use it in contrast with coarser and more linear succulents. The variegated selection adds color interest but may look a little lost among coarser plants.

- **Rhipsalis**—Most rhipsalis look like green waterfalls or mop heads: a mass of green lines rushing from a hanging basket or tall pot. A large hanging basket looks like a giant wig, while a smaller plant emerging from a container suggests a billy goat's beard or goatee. Few other plants—with the exception of grasses—are so full of lines, but these hang down.

- **Sedum**—Tough plants that offer color, line, form, space, and texture. I think sedums provide more for a designer to work with than any other succulent genus. Some cover the "ground" in a pot (*S. acre* and *S. xrubrotinctum*); others produce long ropes that hang or cascade (*S. morganianum* and *S. rupestre* 'Angelina'); and others make fleshy, sturdy mounds of different heights (*S. cauticola*, *S.* 'Herbstfreude', *S. sieboldii*, and *S. spathulifolium* 'Cape Blanco'). Colors range from green to red to gray to yellow to purple to pink, and that applies to the flow-

7

ers almost as much as it does to the foliage. Don't garden in the sun without them!

- **Sempervivum**—Rosette-forming hens and chicks, which are much more cold hardy than their bigger yet more elegant cousins the echeverias, can grow as thick as thieves and create the impression of pointy green lava spilling out of strawberry pots or low bowls. Use the larger ones as starburst accents in a mixed pot, and let the smaller, more prolific selections quickly fill large areas of "ground."

⑥ Many sedums, such as *Sedum telephium* ssp. *ruprechtii,* are hardy in much of North America; the cold they receive during winter dormancy promotes strong growth the next season.

⑦ Not all succulents are small and solid-looking. Members of the genus *Cussonia* can become quite large and offer light feathery foliage.

16: climbers and trailers

Far more than any other group discussed in this book, climbers (plants that use other plants or supports to grow upward naturally) and trailers (those that grow along the ground or have a lax, graceful habit) can be thought of primarily in terms of one design element: line. Many provide colorful flowers and foliage and others offer intriguing textures, yet it is their ability to be trained into lines and linear forms (climbers) or their naturally linear growth habit (trailers) that offers endless design potential for container gardeners. If you want a container planting to direct a viewer's eye vertically (either upward or downward), horizontally, or in an arching or circular manner, consider employing climbers and trailers first.

In more concrete terms, if you would like to raise the height of a container planting without placing the pot on an inverted pot, flight of steps, or plinth, construct a simple teepee from bamboo poles and raffia directly in the pot, or insert an elegant wooden trellis or wrought-iron frame. Then allow a climber to twist its way up the support, or periodically tie a suitably flexible trailer to the frame; in time, you will have added as much height as you wish. Maybe you would rather create a cascade of color flowing from a window box. If so, include climbers and trailers with other plants (if any). Would you like to make a container planting appear to cover more square footage than just the surface area of the pot? Include some trailers, which stretch out and increase the width of a planting without needing to root along the ground. A row of hanging baskets overflowing with climbers and trailers will create a visually irresistible line of sight; when placed closely together, the baskets create a suspended screen. Finally, if you truly want to impress your gardening friends, train a climber onto a wire hoop, sphere, or other form to create a memorable piece of living sculpture.

The adaptability of climbers and trailers does not end there. You can carefully train, tie, and clip a climber into a buttoned-down, very formal-looking shape. Alternatively, you can let the plant go where it will along a frame or perhaps into other plants in the pot or near it. All climbers can be trained with some effort on the part of the gardener, but by the same token, any climber lacking some sort of support will grow downward from a pot or hanging basket (and those in the list of climbers provided all look good

❶ Morning glories (shown here is *Ipomoea acuminata*) climb rapidly and produce abundant blooms. Go easy on the nitrogen fertilizer, though: Too much will result in few blooms and rampant foliage.

❷ Trailing petunias, such as this *Petunia integrifolia,* and the related *Calibrachoa* are both available in a huge color range and can grow quite large in relatively small pots.

- **Cissus**—Familiar grape ivy *(C. rhombifolia)* quickly and easily provides a great many green diamonds (look at the individual leaflets to see what I mean), while *C. discolor*, sometimes called rex begonia vine, offers the stuff of a designer's dream: fantastic silver-marked, rich green, elongate leaves with red-purple undersides on gracefully hanging and curving stems. Don't let it grow too densely, or you will lose the space between the leaves and stems and diminish the foliage impact.

- **Clematis**—Don't be afraid to try a clematis in a pot. Give it a suitable support, such as a trellis or even a hoop, and keep the potting mix moist and out of hot, drying

doing so). Why *not* let a morning glory tumble out of an earthbound pot or aerial hanging basket?

Climbers can present a few challenges, especially to the anal-retentive and time-challenged among us. If you want a climber to cover a support neatly and precisely, then be prepared to periodically wind, tie, and/or clip it to make it bend to your will. Failure to do so will result in a neat-freak's nightmare, with shoots jumping willy-nilly from one part of a support to another or even twisting around their companions.

As with every plant, try to determine the growth rate and potential size of your climber or trailer. Some of these—especially among the tropicals—can cover many linear or square feet in a season or two, while others may extend only a couple of feet, if that. Don't try to grow a morning glory or passionflower in a six-inch pot, and be prepared to include several smaller growers, such as dichondra or lobelia, in a monumental hanging basket.

③ Most ivies grow lustily, so keep them separate or be prepared to restrain them. Some variegated selections, such as *Hedera canariensis* 'Gloire de Marengo', can take on pinkish tints with the onset of cooler weather.

④ Give *Ipomoea batatas* 'Margarita' and other ornamental sweet potatoes plenty of water, fertilizer, and root room to produce cape-like masses of trailing foliage, or restrain them for less abundant but still showy chains.

sun; then enjoy the colorful stars, pinwheels, and bells that appear among usually medium-textured foliage on slender stems. Clematis are often brittle, so shelter them from strong wind.

- **Ficus pumila**—Younger plants of creeping fig project an intricate, fine texture when clinging to a wall, and they can do the same when hanging out of a container or trained onto a support. Train a few plants onto a wire hoop, globe, or other three-dimensional form to produce a specimen plant loaded with visual interest provided by all five design elements. Variegated and miniature-leaved selections offer even more to look at but tend to grow much more slowly than the plain green species.

- **Hedera helix**—I consider English ivy my first candidate for best all-around climber for containers. Hundreds of selections offer a range of colors, leaf forms, and textures, and almost all hang gracefully from a container or lend themselves to training on a form. A few are very cold hardy,

⑤

produces little red "morning glories" on delicate, fine-textured but vigorous vines.

- **Mandevilla**—Although they may take a year or two to reach a statement-making size, they are worth the wait. *Mandevilla xamoena* 'Alice du Pont' bears animated morning-glory-like pink blooms throughout warm and hot weather on twining, fairly coarse vines. Allow plenty of room in the container for one of these. Others, sometimes considered members of the genus *Dipladenia*, tend to be less rambunctious and make suitable additions for smaller containers. Look for these with red, pink, or white flowers and red-toned new growth.

- **Muehlenbeckia**—Fast, fine-textured, and fascinating with its tiny, crown-shaped, Gummi-bear-like white fruits, an angel vine *(M. complexa)* can be trained on virtually anything or can be left to dangle from its container. Impatient gardeners take note: it provides seemingly instant gratification.

- **Passiflora**—Passionflowers should be featured prominently in any depiction of the Garden of Eden: they are lush, sensuous, and so tempting to touch. Vigorous plants produce abundant leaves in a variety of shapes, but the flowers are built mostly on the same exquisite plan of fringed stars with a central cluster of exclamation points. *P. vitifolia* produces vibrant red blooms over a long season. Unlike most of its relatives, blue-lavender *P. caerulea* tolerates quite a bit of cold.

but most benefit from overwintering indoors out of the worst cold weather. Try bright yellow 'Amber Waves', white-painted 'Calico', and fine-textured, busy-looking 'Needlepoint'.

- **Ipomoea**—Late-blooming moonflowers *(I. alba)* open their giant white, morning-glory-like trumpets as night approaches, bringing spots of light to the night and attracting people and moths with their heavenly scent. Think of the now widely available selections of *I. batatas* as English ivies on steroids: big, boisterous, wildly colorful, and rather coarse, but endlessly useful in larger containers. 'Ace of Spades' and 'Blackie' bring a strong suggestion of shadows to sunny spots, 'Margarita' offers dazzling chartreuse and gold, and 'Sweet Caroline' combines variable decorator shades of brown and bronze and purple. Cardinal climber, *I.* x*multifida*,

⑤ The surreal-looking flowers captivate anyone who takes the time to examine a *Passiflora* 'Incense'.

⑥ "Superplant" is not an undeserved moniker for *Scaevola aemula,* which blooms abundantly and quickly bounces back from severe wilting.

- **Rhodochiton atrosanguineus**— You will not find another plant that looks quite like this: a mass of dark green, heart-shaped leaves festooned with dusky purple "bells" with almost black "clappers." Its medium to fine texture stands in bold contrast to the brooding flowers. Blooms the first year from seed where happy, which in my experience is in cool-summer areas, such as the Pacific Northwest and coastal Maine.

- **Solanum jasminoides**—Grow potato vine for its profusion of medium-textured foliage, especially the golden-variegated selection, and for the pretty, blue-white or white starry flowers. Expect a small, well-tended plant to put on at least three feet of growth in one season.

- **Thunbergia alata**—Black-eyed Susan vines are easy to grow and always seem to have at least a few cheerful, five-parted blooms decorating the pointy foliage. Most selections bear flowers in shades of orange, yellow, and white with central black "eyes." Those that do not have black eyes miss the whole

7

point of their charm. There are many other species of *Thunbergia* in many flower colors, but most would prove too much to manage in all but very large containers.

A SELECTION OF TRAILERS FOR CONTAINERS

- **Bacopa (Sutera) 'Snowflake'**— Written about and commercially available under two genus names, this small but mighty workhorse delivers all season by producing hundreds of starry little white flowers above rather fine-textured foliage. Other selections have recently become available with bigger flowers and are worth a try.

- **Dichondra argentea**—Without question one of the top peacemakers for separating two or more potentially conflicting colors. Started from a few small plants, a fine-textured curtain of silver—

yes, it actually looks silver, particularly when sunlight bounces off the leaves—can hide a pot or dangle gracefully from a hanging basket in a few months' time. Look for 'Silver Falls'.

- **Helichrysum petiolare**—Formerly my favorite finer-textured gray-silver trailer until I discovered *Dichondra argentea*, licorice plant still deserves its role as a harmonizer for many other colors. Actually a shrub, it grows quickly and gently curves out from its container, contributing a pleasing line

and spreading form. Chartreuse 'Limelight' deserves your consideration too.

- **Lantana**—One of the very first plants I remember growing was a hot-colored selection of *L. camara*. Most of the kinds available today are still in that color range; for white and lavender, choose selections of *L. montevidensis*. In contrast to the gently outward-arching *L. camara*, *L. montevidensis* is a weeper, hanging straight down from its container or nearly so from the trunk of a standard

7 Whether brilliantly or subtly colored, the flower clusters of *Lantana* attract another purveyor of color: butterflies.

8 A little bit of baby's tears (*Soleirolia soleirolii*) grows rapidly among other plants. Once it reaches the edge of the pot it will cascade down in a fine green rush.

duce long chains of little, rounded leaves that are golden in sun and chartreuse to almost plain green in shade. Little golden flowers appear briefly in summer but do not bring much to the party, I believe. A knockout with deep-toned selections of foliage plants such as *Carex*, *Euphorbia cotinifolia*, *Hemigraphis*, *Solenostemon* (*Coleus*), *Strobilanthes*, and *Tradescantia* (to name a few).

- **Pelargonium peltatum**—Ivy-leaved geraniums are not quite the challenge they once were in regions with hot summers, now that breeders are releasing more heat-tolerant selections. Of course, gardeners in regions with cooler summers can enjoy these all season. Starlike foliage (gold-netted in 'The Crocodile', but the color fades with the onset of heat) produces the backdrop for clusters of flowers that look just like those on bedding geraniums. The advantage here is that they appear on billowing, cascading plants

9   A few stems of *Tradescantia pallida* 'Purpurea' provide linear interest when trailing out of a pot, but a mass of it causes a scene.

topiary. All have sharply scented foliage, which some noses enjoy and others detest.

- **Lobelia erinus**—Fine-textured, low-growing, trailing selections bear masses of flowers in jewel tones of blue, pink, lilac, and white over a long season if you can keep them moist and cool. In warmer areas, enjoy their elfin beauty until heat and drought claim them.

- **Lotus berthelotii**—Certainly one of the finest-textured of all plants suitable for containers, parrot's beak provides a mass of gray-green threadlike foliage to cover the "ground" or cascade from a container. Overfertilization may lessen the silvery gray impact of the leaves. Gardeners in favorable locations enjoy the bright red, curved flowers.

- **Lysimachia nummularia 'Aurea'**—Without question, golden creeping Jenny holds a place on my top-ten list of plants for containers. A hardy perennial, it seems to quickly and effortlessly pro-

instead of on sticks.

- **Petunia**—Talk about a makeover: once dowdy and martyrs to heavy rain, petunias now take their place among the boldest and sturdiest plants for containers. Even the pastel-colored, large-flowered, frilly selections have more oomph these days. Look for the deeply saturated colors of the 'Wave' series as well as stridently magenta *P. integrifolia*, constantly adorned with little trumpets with black "eyes" even if you forget to water it occasionally. Some selections have a gentle fragrance, and all but the smallest flowers clamp down on your nose when you take a good whiff. Try it.

- **Plectranthus**—Lots of useful, vigorous trailers here, including bold-textured, slightly stiff-looking, silvery gray *P. argentatus;* precisely white-edged *P. forsteri* 'Marginatus'; and several others that travel under a welter of confused and conflicting names. Almost all of the latter group luxuriate in warm and hot weather and bear sticky-fuzzy, pungently scented foliage. Perhaps the most useful is a dark green selection of *P. coleoides* with dark red undersides. It combines with everything.

- **Salvia discolor**—Another silver trailer (I really like them, can you tell?), but this one has gray upper and almost white, fuzzy lower leaf surfaces, and it looks quite open. The flowers come close to being black, but don't grow *S. discolor* solely for that reason: the flowers do not pack nearly as much punch as the foliage.

- **Scaevola aemula**—Let's all thank Australia for producing this champion. 'Blue Wonder' and similar selections bear fanlike clusters of similarly fanlike flowers for months. By season's end, a planting of this at the top of a wall at a friend's nursery had produced a traffic-stopping, three-foot-long, violet-blue shower of constant color. Don't garden without it.

- **Tradescantia pallida 'Purpurea'**— Unlike anything else on this list, 'Purpurea' (also known as 'Purple Heart') creates an energetic, sprawling mass of bladelike, dark purple foliage, especially when grown "hard" (in plenty of sun and in smallish containers that are allowed to go a bit dry before watering). Pinkish violet flowers add a whimsical touch to the drama.

- **Verbena**—Most verbena hybrids bear flower clusters that look like brooches in shades of red, purple, white, and peach. The blooms appear all season on vigorous, spreading plants, and some are lightly fragrant. While most verbenas have low-key, medium-textured foliage, the selections of *V. tenuisecta* (aptly called moss verbena) offer very fine leaves that give the effect of a wispy green cloud.

17: perennials

I can imagine the questions as you read the title of this section: Why on earth would anyone want to grow herbaceous perennials in containers when there are plenty of perfectly good places for them in borders? Do they bloom long enough and have foliage that merits their space in a pot? Do they actually grow well enough in a container to produce a nice display? If they do grow well, won't they die over winter unless I give them really special treatment? After all, I spent good money on these plants, and I don't want to throw them away at the end of the season like I do my annuals.

It's true: growing perennials in containers requires thinking outside the disposable-annuals box, but the rewards often compensate for the extra thought and effort. First,

consider the season-long appearance of a perennial, much as you do when you include a perpetually colorful coleus or an endlessly blooming verbena in a planting. Very few perennials naturally bloom over an extended period (as many annuals do, of course), so let's not fault them for that quality. Instead, direct your evaluation to the foliage. Does the foliage remain attractive all season, or does it become unsightly as the plant prepares to go dormant in summer? Do pest depredations or the natural processes of growth (such as leaves turning yellow) require a great deal of effort to keep the plants growing healthily and looking good? Admittedly, some perennials probably do need to remain in a border for failing to meet these criteria: favorites such as tall bearded irises, delphiniums, Oriental poppies, yarrows, old-fashioned bleeding hearts, and columbines are probably better managed where other plants can disguise their shortcomings in a much larger setting. However, plenty of perennials offer handsome foliage all season, are not normally bothered excessively by pests, and do not take too much

effort to keep them participating as a worthy member of a container planting.

I spend time helping out and just plain puttering at a local nursery, and I have learned that a great many perennials do quite well in containers. After all, the plants must remain in their pots until a buyer takes them away to plant them in the open ground. Plenty of perennials spend at least a year in a pot (sometimes more than one as the plant grows and needs more room), and they remain in very good condition, providing their cultural needs are met. Because

① If your container plantings lack linear interest, look no farther than *Phormium* 'Color Guardsman' for the solution, beautifully paired here with *Geum* 'Red Wings'.

② Though a sub-tropical native, *Phygelius* 'Baby Drops' can be grown in mild climates as a perennial and as a tender perennial in colder climes.

they can potentially live longer than an annual, potted perennials require a more substantial potting mix if they are to succeed. Instead of a fine-textured mix high in peat, which will decompose by season's end, plant perennials in a coarser mix composed of ground bark, coir, compost, or similar large-particled material. Real garden soil added to a perennial potting mix helps preserve the structural integrity of the mix and also holds nutrients well. Speaking of nutrients, perennials need nutrients like any other container plant, and they all have their own needs for quality and quantity. Learn what they are and provide them for best results.

Yes, if you want to overwinter perennials you must foster their survival. Cold-hardy plants must be given a cold period to grow well the next year, but don't think this means they can remain outdoors all winter in their pot aboveground. A ball of coarse-textured potting mix in an exposed pot freezes more quickly than the same volume of real soil in open ground, and by the same token it thaws more quickly, too. The double whammy of more-rapid freezing

and thawing wreaks havoc on roots, not only from direct cold damage to the tissues, but also from physical damage from the up-and-down tearing action of heaving and dropping as water freezes (and expands) and melts (thereby shrinking back to its original volume). If you live in an area where freezing temperatures persist for a few weeks or more, and you know that the root balls of your plants can tolerate being frozen, try to keep frozen root balls that way. It is better than the roller coaster freeze-and-thaw ride.

In most areas, hardy perennials need some sort of protection to keep them alive over winter, so be prepared to take appropriate measures. Otherwise, you can treat perennials as (in many cases) expensive annuals and replace them the next year. However, many perennials grown in containers increase in stature and beauty over the years, so it makes sense to at least try to protect them during winter. And

3 A stately pot of lily of the Nile (*Agapanthus*) commands attention even in a complicated setting. Keep the congested clumps in their pots until they appear to be lifting themselves out; they should bloom abundantly until then.

③

don't forget that one original plant can become several in a year or two; dividing the clump results in more plants to garden with and often more than recovers the cost of the initial investment.

Perennials provide endless raw material for adventures with color, line, form, space, and texture, as the following list demonstrates. Besides, won't your gardening friends and family be impressed as they marvel at creative and sophisticated combination pots of hostas and coleus or bamboo and basil?

A SELECTION OF PERENNIALS FOR CONTAINERS

- **Agapanthus**—This perennial has everything: blue or white globes of lilylike flowers borne on tall, linear stems well above an arching mass of medium-textured, grasslike leaves. Selections are best grown by themselves and moved to larger pots as the roots build up and almost break the pot. Use them as focal points or as a temporary massed feature around a pool or pond when in bloom.

- **Bergenia**—These plants give an impression similar to hostas, but they go one step further by being evergreen. Lusty, rounded, thick leaves provide coarse texture all season, and many feature red or purple tints during cold weather. Congested clusters of flowers in white and shades of pink add to the weighty, substantial feeling.

- **Carex**—Sedges have the same visual qualities of many clump-forming grasses but generally tolerate much wetter conditions. They offer a great deal of contrasting color, line, and texture to a mixed planting. I particularly like the bronzy selections, such as *C. comans*

'Bronze Form' and *C. flagellifera*. A new one (to me, anyway), *C.* 'Milk Chocolate', sounds intriguing.

- **Chrysanthemum**—Of course you can head out to the roadside stand or nursery in fall to pick up a few spectacular pots of chrysanthemums to drop into bare spots.

④ Sometimes flowers aren't necessary to provide plenty of interest. *Farfugium japonicum* 'Argenteum' grows best with plenty of moisture and protection from strong, hot sunlight.

⑤ The almost mirror-like surface of many *Bergenia* leaves begs further inspection. Gently rub a leaf, and you'll discover why 'Bressingham Ruby' is commonly called Pigsqueak.

⑤

However, if you are looking for a different color on a less massively flowered and stiff-looking mound, search out *C.* 'Sheffield' (sometimes listed as *Dendranthema*). Late in the season, its open mass of dark green foliage acts as a perfect foil for daisylike flower heads of pinkish apricot, not a color you would expect in fall, certainly not from a mum.

- **Farfugium japonicum**—Once part of the genus *Ligularia,* these are superb coarse-textured foliage plants, whether combined as young divisions with other plants in the same pot or allowed to build up over time into stunning specimens. The wavy and cut edges of some forms lighten the texture, as do the spots or splashes of yellow or white on others.

- **Ferns**—I do not think I have ever seen an ugly fern. As a group they offer all five design elements and a range of qualities within each one; there are very tender as well as bone-hardy ones; some grow in sun instead of shade; and you can choose from ones barely a few inches high to several feet or more.

Look for many great container plants among *Adiantum, Asplenium, Athyrium, Dicksonia* (tree ferns), *Dryopteris, Nephrolepis, Lygodium* (climbing ferns), *Osmunda,* and *Pteris,* to name some of my favorites.

- **Grasses/Bamboos**—Like ferns, grasses and their bamboo relatives offer all five design elements in spades, but their chief claim to fame is their elegance of line. They are not all stereotypically "grassy" in appearance,

though: witness the bamboos and *Arundo donax* (giant reed). Be sure to provide a pot big enough to accommodate them for a season or two before repotting or dividing them. Favorite perennial grasses for contain-

⑥ Plant a hardy *Athyrium nipponicum* 'Pictum', or Japanese painted fern, in a shaded container as a light-textured background for other blooms.

⑦ Got deer? Those four-legged eating machines might not devour your prized hostas if grown in containers near your house or on a second-story deck.

ers include *Arundo, Hakonechloa,* and smaller *Miscanthus* selections, and by all means look for *Rhynchelytrum repens,* which starts out looking like crabgrass and then sends out showy, dark red flowers. Among the bamboos, try *Arundinaria, Fargesia,* and *Sasa.*

- **Gunnera manicata**—Worth growing exclusively for its spectacle value: picture cut-edged, rounded leaves up to six feet across on equally robust stems (and if that does not work for you, think of a gigantic rhubarb). It probably will not attain those dimensions in a pot, but it will still be big. Check its water needs daily, especially during hot, dry weather. Ask a friend to help you move it in and out of winter storage, and show your gratitude by providing a nice lunch.

- **Helleborus**—Hellebores have become one of the "It" plants beloved by everyone from gardening cognoscenti to everyday dirt gardeners, and with good reason. They offer simple yet intriguing, very early-blooming flowers in an ever-widening range of mostly

muted colors; their leaves offer eye-catching lines and form; the foliage contains space with the leaflets and defines more space between the leaves; and textures range within the broad midsection of the continuum. And they do very well in containers.

• **Hosta**—Tough as nails when grown in pots, hostas offer an abundance of foliage colors (including a zillion shades of green as well as yellow and blue, plus white and even red) that occur with the basic frame-

work of mounded rosettes. Texture leans overall toward the coarse side, but there are plenty of medium-coarse examples as well. A few feature attractive flowers, but (I believe) in most cases the flowers spoil the appear-

⑧ If you haven't discovered hellebores yet, or yours are relegated to your beds and borders, by all means try a few in pots. Grow them by themselves, then repot them into a fresh mix every other year.

⑨ Also discussed as a climber (page 202), some perennial clematis can give a container dramatic height, such as this *Clematis xrecta* 'Seriously Black'.

ance of the plants and are best cut off and taken inside for enjoyment as cut flowers. Grow them to splendor by themselves in their pots, and then group them with other plants to stunning effect.

- **Lamium and Lamiastrum**—Great fillers and gentle cascaders, dead nettles offer abundant and pleasant foliage, often marked with silver. Perky flower clusters come in shades of yellow, purple, and white. These plants look best interacting with others in combination pots, but be prepared to remove them every year for division and replanting.

- **Liriope**—Plants of this genus look like some grasses but produce flower clusters resembling white or purple grape hyacinths (*Muscari*), to which they are related. Unlike most grasses, lilyturf remains a low mound throughout the season. Both the clumping *L. muscari* and running *L. spicata* grow well in containers, either by themselves as specimens or adding a linear quality to combination pots. Although evergreen to semievergreen, they look best if cut down to an inch or two above the crowns in early spring; fresh, clean-looking new foliage (attractively variegated in some forms) will replace the tattered old leaves.

- **Mentha**—Frankly, this is one of the few genera that belong exclusively in a pot, unless you do not mind it taking over large areas of your garden. Mints spread like wildfire via underground runners; in favorable soil (which is almost anything but bone dry and poor), a mint can "walk" several feet in only a few years. But don't deny yourself the pleasure of enjoying the clean fragrances, bright to dark green coloration, and upright

lines of mints: grow them in a pot with a drainage hole covered by a piece of screen (they can escape out of an unscreened hole into the freedom of the open garden) or on a stone slab, and rub the leaves as you walk by. Mint juleps, anyone?

- **Ophiopogon jaburan**—Think of these as mostly smaller versions of their cousins in the genus *Liriope*. Two standouts are *O. jaburan* 'Vittatus' (with white-edged leaves and jewel-like blue fruit) and *O. planiscapus* 'Nigrescens'

(a low-growing beauty with very dark, almost black leaves). Use the former to create the illusion of light on the "ground level" of a container planting and the latter to suggest shadows at the base of taller plants.

- **Phormium**—Grasslike plants with attitude from Down Under: many are big, arching mounds of strapping foliage, often variegated in light or sunset shades. Grow them as specimens to contrast with more rounded and broader forms. Northern growers, be patient: they grow slowly in areas with long winters, but a plant can live in the same roomy pot for several years.
- **Polygonatum odoratum 'Variegatum'**—All of the larger-growing Solomon's seals have the same basic ladderlike arrangement of leaves along arching stems and short-lived, dangling bell-like

⑩ A pleasant-looking trailer for the edge of a roomy pot, *Lamium galeobdolon* 'Hermann's Pride' also looks splendid when grown as a mass.

⑪ Purple moor grass (here, *Molinia caerulea* 'Variegata') makes a charming cascade from a traditional cast-iron urn in Thomas Hobbs' garden in Vancouver, BC.

flowers, but this one adds a fine line of cream along the edges of the leaves. To me, a good-sized clump of this by itself in a pot looks like a gushing green fountain. A few stems in a combination pot provide a nice contrast to mounds and straight linear forms and echo the line of trailing cohabitants.

• **Saxifraga stolonifera**—While many perennials in this list assertively express themselves, this little ground-hugger adds a note of subtlety. Round leaves in loose

rosettes provide an attractive repeating pattern, particularly when the plant is allowed to follow its reproductive urges and send out stolons, which produce new plants. Place a few plants near the rim of a pot to let a few stolons dangle over the edge. 'Tricolor' adds a strong note of pink to the species' dark green leaves with red-purple undersides. White flowers on tall, thin stalks look like insects in flight.

• **Stachys byzantina**—Plant a few lamb's ears in a pot in spring, and by fall you should have a small flock of them. Almost everything about this plant suggests a quiet, restful softness: muted, silvery green leaves, not much line activity, no distinctive form, no space between the leaves, and a texture right in the middle of the range. It is quite literally soft, too: run your fingers along the woolly leaves to understand the significance of the common name. 'Primrose Heron' looks the same, except clothed in a mysterious combination of grayed chartreuse to gold.

18: tropicals

As with many broadly encompassing terms, "tropical plant" means different things to different people. Most would agree that a tropical plant grows natively in the geographical area referred to as the tropics, but that is where horticultural harmony usually ends. Many cacti and other succulents hail from regions that lie between the Tropic of Cancer and the Tropic of Capricorn, yet few would grow them as they would a begonia or banana. The species behind many garden annuals, such as coleus and impatiens, were introduced to temperate regions from the tropics, but they are often not thought of as tropicals, either. Other tropical plants, including cannas and caladiums, often get lumped in with bulbs and similar plants for horticultural purposes (as they are in this book).

Because they share a strong linear quality with other climbers and trailers, the tropical plants that would otherwise be included in this chapter appear in Chapter 16. The plants presented as tropicals in this chapter might be considered as the leftovers from a process of categorizing plants for cultural and design purposes, but that would sell them short. However grouped, tropical plants often serve as both the divas and the backup singers of container plantings.

Like perennials, trees and shrubs, and some bulbs, tropicals promise more than one annual season of enjoyment. Many improve with age, and sooner or later they require pruning, division, and other tasks routinely performed on longer-lasting plants. One of those tasks, namely overwintering, becomes a fork in the road for anyone who gardens in a region that experiences the frosts of fall and spring and the cold of winter. Confronted with the realities of schlepping plants and pots inside and providing appropriate indoor care until the plants can be returned to their warm-weather havens, some

① Most abutilons will continue to bloom over winter if kept under warm and bright cover and moderately watered.

② Plant *Euphorbia cotinifolia* in a light-colored container to pick up on the pale bark of its older stems and provide contrast with the rich red leaves.

gardeners abandon their tropicals at the end of the season. Let's not look down our horticultural noses at those folks; they have their reasons for their practices. However, many tropicals are easily overwintered by letting them go dormant (or nearly so) and storing them in surprisingly cool places, such as a basement or minimally heated garage, greatly saving on heating costs and precious greenhouse space. Readers in warmer zones no doubt smile as they read these words, since their tropicals take a brief winter rest or simply keep going year-round.

Here is a trick that works for tropicals no matter where you grow them: mulch them with a slow-release pelleted fertilizer. Yes, mulch them. The photographer for this book has introduced many people to his practice of pushing tropicals to their limits by covering the surface of the potting mix with an inch or so of a pelleted fertilizer. The actions of summer rain and heat and additional waterings—often delivering a water-soluble fertilizer—release the nutrients into the mix and allow the plants to attain impressive stature by season's end. A little personal experimentation will indicate how much more or less than an inch of pellets will work for you.

Whatever the costs and effort, gardeners should employ at least a few tropicals in their container gardening. With shapes and colors mindful of Paul Gauguin and Peter Max, they bring a lush, exotic, perhaps primeval feeling to gardens from Fairbanks to Fort Lauderdale, and one carefully chosen specimen can enliven even the smallest of spaces.

A SELECTION OF TROPICALS FOR CONTAINERS

- **Abutilon**—Flowering maples, so-called because their leaves resemble the foliage of true maples (*Acer*), offer textural interest as well as dancing lamp- or bell-like flowers in white, pink, and many shades of hot colors. Grow them as exuberant shrubs or quickly and easily train them into impressive topiaries. They fill in rapidly after being cut back hard at the beginning of the growing season. *Abutilon pictum* 'Thompsonii' is a favorite, producing pink-orange flowers and rich green leaves assertively marked with yellow.

- **Acalypha**—I invite you to try to find two identical leaves on almost any selection of *A. wilkesiana:* between the splashes of bright and dark colors, randomly cut edges, and rolled or twisted shapes, the foliage offers a party on every plant. *Acalypha hispida*, on the other hand, produces sedate, almost coarse, plain green leaves,

which provide a backdrop for the masses of red, chenillelike flower chains that dangle straight down from the stems. Don't cut these back too hard; they grow more slowly than many tropicals.

- **Asparagus**—Use asparagus ferns for their delicate texture and lively green color, especially *A. densiflorus* 'Myersii', which makes dramatically arching, tail-like stems that define large triangular spaces between them. Grow it as a specimen to enjoy its sculptural quality and to contrast it with weaker, less distinctly defined shapes. Climbing or flopping *A. scandens* provides a completely different look, with engagingly twisting stems and misty foliage.

- **Begonia**—The rex begonia group includes some of the lushest-looking and flashiest of all plants, mak-

❸ Even when the leaves of *Ensete ventricosum* 'Maurelii' are shredded by the wind or assaulted by chewing insects, they remain intriguing.

❹ The genus *Alternanthera* offers a huge range of colorful leaves on mostly compact plants; *A. dentata* 'Tricolor' is one of the extroverts.

ing slowly expanding mounds of intensely colorful, often metallic-looking leaves that remind me of swirling skirts. The much faster-growing cane-stem types (often called angel-wing begonias) resemble erupting geysers of winglike leaves, often spotted with shiny silver, red, or pink. Cane-stems also produce clusters of (usually) pink or orange flowers, sometimes almost the size of your head. Don't overwater any of these, and keep them out of strong sun and wind.

- **Bromeliads**—Almost every bromeliad follows the basic pattern of a dynamic starburst of thick leaves, but don't think they are all the same: look for solid green ones or selections with intricate patterns of almost black, yellow, white, and silver, and many appear to have pink or red "fingernails" at the leaf tips. Flowers in many strong,

⑤ Expect Angel's trumpets (*Brugmansia*) to bloom in cycles—and to anxiously await the peaks and mourn the valleys.

⑥ Cane-stem tropical begonias come in a huge variety of shapes and leafy colors, with foliage that ranges from gold to green, fuzzy to shiny, and spotted to striped.

almost neon shades emerge from sturdy protective bracts, often of a highly contrasting color. In time, some selections build up into impressive clusters of many individual plants. All of them offer all five design elements in abundance. Look for *Aechmea, Ananas, Cryptanthus, Dyckia, Guzmania, Neoregelia, Tillandsia,* and *Vriesia,* among others.

• **Brugmansia**—Big, arching and spreading plants bear large but usually unassertive leaves that let the trumpetlike flowers stand out. To me they do not look like trumpets as much as flowing, floor-length gowns in white, pink, yellow, and apricot. Most emit a sweet, mesmerizing fragrance that floats on the air in the evening. Heavy watering and fertilizing can produce a six-foot plant from a six-inch start in one season, so give it plenty of room. If I could grow only one, it would be apricot-colored 'Charles Grimaldi'.

- **Chlorophytum comosum**—Yes, the plain old and very familiar spider plant from every dorm room and wraparound porch belongs on my list of favorites. Both the all-green and white-striped selections offer an abundance of arching lines and animated mounds. Let the baby spiders parachute from a basket or allow them to dangle from an earthbound combination planting. And don't forget to share some babies with your friends.

- **Codiaeum**—Crotons, with their bright splashes of color and elongated, outward-moving leaves, offer a strong suggestion of Mardi Gras to any planting. They are not quiet, and some of their colors do not play well with others, but few plants suggest the tropics as these do. Like acalyphas, they are fairly slow but steady, so don't bushwhack them unless they get too big.

7 *Cordyline australis* 'Pink Stripe' is a favorite in potted compositions, as a vertical accent or grouped for a study in warm lines.

8 After the leaves die back in fall, give *Musa zebrina* (or its kin) a dribble of water occasionally in a cool, dimly lit spot, and it will resume growth as it wakes up in the spring.

- **Cordyline australis**—One word: line. All cordylines look like they are exploding, whether as individual fireworks from a specimen pot or as part of a bigger display that combines several pots. Some come in solid green and others dark red, and many are powerfully striped with yellow, pink, or white. Use them sparingly as accents or group several together: You will almost believe you can hear cymbals clashing from behind them.

- **Cycads**—Cycads can best be described as giant ferns, although most cannot be described as delicate. Primarily rich, dark green, a few (particularly *Encephalartos horridus*) offer shades of bluish gray. They provide very strong lines, definite forms, and a clear presence of space, and they almost always grow and look best as solitary specimens. Note: Cycads are slow growing and many are becoming very rare in the wild, so try to determine the origin of a specimen you are thinking about buying, especially a big one. Look for *Cycas*, *Encephalartos*, and *Zamia*.

- **Dracaena**—Think of these as mostly smaller, less assertive cordylines. Selections of *D. marginata*, often referred to as "spikes" in the nursery trade, bring color and line to many plantings. Consider thinking outside the spike box by placing more than one in a pot or planting one off-center or with the stem at an angle.
- **Duranta erecta**—*Duranta* produces mostly rather plain-looking foliage on average-looking plants, but selections shine when in bloom and can be the star of the show in fruit. Hanging clusters of flowers in white or variations of blue and purple mature to open bunches of very showy yellow fruit that give the plant its common name, golden dewdrop. A brilliant gold-leafed form remains low and dense and turns a very appealing chartreuse when protected from strong sun.
- **Euphorbia cotinifolia**—Seek this one out: Smallish, wine-colored leaves resembling those of smokebush (*Cotinus*) elegantly stand out from beige-colored stems. It is sensational when used with orange and yellow and even stronger shades of blue and purple, and see what happens when you combine this with anything chartreuse. A small plant will become a good-sized shrub in a few years, so give it some space. Avoid remaining in prolonged contact with the white, latexlike sap: Like many of its relatives, this euphorbia can produce pain-

ful reactions, especially if it comes in contact with your eyes, nose, or mouth.
- **Ferns (including tree ferns)**—Like their hardier perennial counterparts (see Chapter 17), the tender tropical ferns provide elegant expressions of all five design elements. Maidenhair ferns (*Adiantum*) look very delicate and fragile, while Boston ferns (*Nephrolepis*) seem robust, and bird's nest fern (*Asplenium nidus*) offers the starburst look of some bromeliads. A planting of one or more tree ferns (*Dicksonia*) recalls the age of dinosaurs.

⑨ In addition to the rex and cane-stem types, the rhizomatous begonias, such as *Begonia soli-mutata,* also offer a full palette of design attributes. Water sparingly during their winter rest.

⑩ With something as visually engaging as *Hibiscus acetosella* 'Coppertone', even a plant grown as a single stem will attract attention. Full sun brings out the best color.

you more éclat among your gardening friends.

- **Musa/Ensete**—One banana plant in a big pot says "tropical" more than a whole bunch of other, less statuesque cohorts. Not big on color (except for some dark-toned and variegated selections), bananas stand out with their strong lines, recognizable form, ample space between their large leaves, and unabashedly coarse texture. Whether from the genus *Musa* or the closely related *Ensete*, any banana makes a powerful contribution to a container planting. For added interest, let a colorful climber use it for support.

- **Hibiscus**—While selections of the large-flowered Chinese or Hawaiian hibiscus (*H. rosa sinensis*) make gorgeous specimen plants and inspiration for endless fabric patterns, the smaller, seldom-flowering *H. acetosella* 'Coppertone' plays a more versatile role in container plantings. Dark purple-red, maplelike leaves emit an iridescent metallic glow in strong sun and provide a robust contrast to both stronger and gentler colors. A frequently pruned standard topiary (its rapid growth can be gangly at times) makes an unfor-gettable specimen plant.

- **Manihot esculenta 'Variegata'**—Be the first on your block to enjoy this fancy version of the plant that produces poi, that gooey stuff served in Hawaii. White- and yellow-splashed starlike leaves on red-tinged stalks erupt from pale, bumpy stems. An unpinched plant will produce a solitary burst of foliage, while pinching out the growing point when the stem reaches a few feet tall will promote a multiheaded conversation piece. It resembles a variegated *Schefflera arboricola*, but this one will give

- **Solanum**—Flashy relatives of potatoes, all of these add a touch of the unusual. *Solanum pyracanthum* offers weakly upright stems and deeply cut foliage bristling with orange thorns, and starry

⑪ *Asparagus densiflorus* 'Myersii' appears to be erupting from a thoughtfully chosen pan container. In time this plant can spread as much as six feet across.

⑫ A creamy variegated cultivar of *Acalypha wilkesii,* a tropical shrub, works well with other greens, blues, and purples.

purple flowers add interest. Pinching makes a more compact and manageable plant, or you can let it flop into its companions. I grow *S. quitoense* strictly for its big, broad-shouldered, supremely coarse leaves armed with wicked purple thorns, although the pale flowers that mature to golf-ball-sized fruits attract attention. *Solanum rantonnetii* is a floppy, unkempt-looking shrub that can be trained into impressive, massive topiaries covered with rich purple, rounded flowers all season.

- **Strobilanthes dyerianus**—Mindful of a sultan's treasure trove, Persian shield brings unapologetic metallic pur-

ple to hot-weather gardening. Dark companions make it stand out even more, while lighter foliage and flowers, especially in lighter shades, seem to jump out against it. Widely spaced, elongated leaves contribute some spatial and linear interest. Not for the fainthearted.

- **Tibouchina**—*Tibouchina urvilleana* offers a textbook-example complementary color combination of assertively green leaves and opulent purple flowers. Impressed leaf veins create a quilted look, and the rather large but often sparsely borne flowers suggest exotic butterflies with purple wings and reddish legs. Similar *T. grandifolia* produces silver-haired foliage and clusters of smaller but equally vibrant purple blooms.

- **Tradescantia**—While all built along the same lines of oblong leaves arranged alternately along arching or trailing stems, different selections provide very different feelings to container plantings. Most interesting of all, I think, is *T. sillamontana,* which looks like silver-haired ladders emerging from a pot or hanging basket and is arguably most attractive grown alone as a specimen.

19: trees and shrubs

If you have accepted the arguments offered for growing perennials in pots, then it will not be that much of a leap to agree with the value of using woody plants—trees and shrubs—as container subjects. As we did with perennials, let's address a few of their potentially negative aspects before moving on to several of their positive ones.

It is obvious that no one is going to attempt to raise a fully grown live oak, sugar maple, or Douglas fir in a pot; even the deepest of pockets cannot drastically alter the sensible practices of pot-making, horticulture, and simple reason. But plenty of woody plants grow to completely manageable dimensions, and quite a few remain as small as (or smaller than) many annuals and perennials. If your garden space can accommodate four- or six- or even ten-foot plants, and you own some containers large enough to accommodate them, then why not consider incorporating a few trees or shrubs into the mix? Also, as long as gardeners have access to pruning shears and saws, even plants with the potential to grow quite large can be restrained, at least for a few years. Consider what bonsai masters have achieved for centuries: their root- and top-pruning techniques can keep a huge plant relatively small for decades and sometimes centuries, so container gardeners can take a page from their ancient book.

It is an indisputable fact that for the price of a well-grown, rather small tree or shrub, a container gardener could buy half a dozen perennials or perhaps several flats of annuals. However, with reasonable care, a tree or shrub will survive for several years in a pot. If you must justify the cost of a tree or shrub to yourself or someone else, put on your accounting hat and view the cost as amortizable over the years that you enjoy a more costly plant (this works for other kinds of plants, as well as for pots). At the end of a few years you will have spent the same amount on one large specimen as you otherwise might have on a number of smaller ones, and many of those smaller ones will probably be long gone.

Since you will not discard a tree or shrub at the end of a season as you probably would an annual and might a perennial, some maintenance issues will need to be addressed. Aside from keeping the plant at a manageable size, woody plants benefit from routine and as-needed pruning, watering, and fertilizing to look their best. Some also require a cold period in winter, and some may require protection or rescue from insects, disease, winter or storm damage, and other perils. Good gardeners perform those tasks for smaller container plants and their inground plants anyway, and it does not require a vastly larger effort to care for trees and shrubs.

Now let's look at some of the pros of using trees and shrubs in your containers. Their potentially greater longevity and long-term economy was alluded to above, but there is more. First and foremost is the unavoidable presence of a relatively large tree or shrub in a container planting: while not necessarily on the magnitude of a nine-hundred-pound gorilla, its dimensions and considerable mass still make a statement. Even when dwarfed by much larger and

① A specimen of corkscrew hazel (*Corylus avellana* 'Contorta') offers one-of-a-kind linear interest. Like many trees and shrubs, it makes a superb container plant if provided routine care over the years.

showier annuals and perennials, most thoughtfully chosen, relatively smaller to diminutive trees and shrubs (such as floribunda roses and dwarf conifers) command attention through their attractive foliage, distinctive coloration, or eye-catching form. Think of them as the backbone of an individual container planting or group of pots—annuals and even perennials may come and go, but a tree or shrub lasts.

Extending the idea of presence, nothing expresses it

more directly in a pot than does a well-tended topiary: think of a nearly perfect sphere of myrtle on a stout stem or a sharply edged boxwood cone. Many trees and shrubs lend themselves to shaping into quite precise geometric forms or at least close approximations. Formally trained plants can create feelings of order and stability. They certainly suggest that the gardener has a green thumb and a disciplined mind.

A note on some choices for topiary: standard topiaries, with their classic "ball on a stick" formal appearance, justifiably take pride of place in many container gardens. Several woody plants not included in the list at the end of this chapter make excellent topiary subjects, including species and selections of *Buxus sempervirens* (boxwood), *Coprosma xkirkii*, *Ilex* (holly), *Laurus nobilis* (bay), *Myrtus communis* (myrtle), *Syzygium paniculatum* (eugenia), and *Westringia rosmarinifolia* (Victorian rosemary).

A well-tended and integrated tree or shrub lends an air of permanence to a container planting. Anyone who recognizes the difference between a marigold and a colored-twig dogwood will perceive some suggestion of age and settledness from the dogwood. If this is a feeling you wish to convey in a planting, then trees and shrubs fit the bill. They might even lend an aristocratic quality to a small suburban patio or deck.

2   Hummingbirds, sphinx moths, and many butterflies will thank you for including Cape fuchsias (*Phygelius*) such as 'Yellow Trumpet' in your container plantings.

3   *Skimmia japonica* can be used in winter pots in mild zones, when its clumps of ruby-colored buds are prevalent before giving way to starry-white, fragrant flowers in March.

Years ago I taught a course on woody plants to a variety of audiences. One technique I drove into my students' heads (at least I hope I did!) was identifying and evaluating the Five Fs of a particular woody plant: foliage, fall color, flowers, fruit, and form, all of which are attractively offered by outstanding trees and shrubs. I also constantly reminded my students to be mindful of a sixth attribute: a plant's bark. Whether gray and ridged, brown and platy, or red and smooth, bark adds another dimension to a woody plant, and that cannot be said of annuals or perennials.

Although not often considered, bark quality can become the memorable, and impressive, icing on the cake. It is one of many reasons why you as a container gardener will now consider using trees and shrubs in containers . . . right?

A SELECTION OF TREES AND SHRUBS FOR CONTAINERS

- **Acer palmatum**—Of all the many maples, I think Japanese maples make the best container subjects. Quite a few of them grow slowly and can be kept even

smaller through judicious pruning. 'Sango-kaku' produces typical starry leaves, which turn a clear yellow in fall, but this one's claim to fame is its almost glowing red bark in winter. All of the cut-leaf forms (*A. palmatum* var. *dissectum* and many named cultivars) produce lacy foliage that ignites in fall; many of them grow into gently weeping, almost flowing mounds.

- **Ajania pacifica**—A close relative of *Chrysanthemum*, *Ajania* is prized far more for its dark green foliage with gray-felted edges and undersides than for its clusters of yellow-button flowers in late fall. It looks best when grown by itself in a pot, which allows the neat mound shape to develop unhindered. Cut back by half in spring to keep it tight, especially if you fertilize liberally.

- **Aloysia triphylla**—I grow lemon verbena primarily for its powerfully lemon-scented foliage, but its fine texture can make a nice

④ Vibrant red-stemmed dogwood (*Cornus sanguinea* 'Midwinter Fire') is perfect for winter pots, even in colder climates.

contrast to coarser leaves. It may fall short in attributes when compared with many other woody plants, but you will not care when you intentionally rub the leaves or unintentionally brush it as you walk by. Try it as an open, informal topiary.

- **Anisodontea xhypomadara**—If you want little hibiscus-like pink blooms on a fine-textured shrub for months, then this is your plant. Grow more than one so that you can get them on a staggered cycle of cutting back, which will keep the plants denser, and at least one should be in bloom at any given time while the others are setting buds. You can also let plants grow looser and more openly, which will let them mix more easily with other plants in a combination pot. It quickly and readily makes a very appealing topiary.

- **Citrus**—Everyone should be able to enjoy the delicious floral fragrance and satisfying plump fruit of citrus. Of course most selections grow rather large, and all of them must be protected in cold areas, but they are worth the effort. My pick of the litter is *C. ichangensis*, a compact grower that periodically bears heavy crops of perfect, average-sized, bright yellow lemons at an early age on quite small plants. Keep it in one of your best pots.

- **Cornus**—Almost all of the colored-twig dogwoods grow large and must be mercilessly thinned out and cut back, but no other group of plants offers such dramatically colorful lines in winter. The smooth bark on selections of *C. alba*, *C. sanguinea*, and *C. stolonifera* offers warming shades of red, yellow, and orange to light up your winter garden, and some variegated selections bring color and medium texture to pots in summer.

- **Cuphea**—Two quite different species make equally valuable contributions to container gardening. *Cuphea hyssopifolia* (Hawaiian heather) produces very fine-textured, intricately branched mounds studded with starry little white or lavender flowers. *Cuphea ignea* (cigar flower) is much more open, with larger, widely spaced leaves and fewer but prominent tubular red flowers that draw hummingbirds and butterflies.

- **Fuchsia**—Those of you who live in areas with mild winters and cooler summers can grow just about any of the hundreds of selections available, so by all means enjoy their candy colors and unique dancing-lady flower form on upright to gracefully cascading plants. A hot, humid summer almost guarantees their demise, except for the triphylla types, most famously represented by upright-growing 'Gartenmeister Bonstedt'. Its dark red-toned foliage and elongated bright orange-red flowers almost make me forget about the other ones.

- **Hebe**—Many of these grow too large for most containers, but you can always tuck a few little-leafed hebes in with coarser-textured plants for a very pleasing contrast. I particularly like *H. xfranciscana* 'Variegata', with cheerful cream-edged leaves and occasional purple flowers.

- **Hydrangea macrophylla**—Yes, those big, zaftig shrubs that thrive by the coast grow quite well by

⑤

themselves in equally big containers. Give them plenty of water and fertilizer for the most abundant display of their magnificent globs of flowers against robust, coarse-textured foliage. Start with 'Endless Summer', a relatively new selection that is taking the gardening world by storm, and for good reason: once it starts blooming, at least a few ethereal blue flower heads will attract attention for the rest of the season.

• **Juniperus**—If you want to have some green (or blue-gray or gold) in your cold-country container garden overwinter, try some selections of *J. chinensis* (Chinese juniper) in big pots. Most grow quite large but can be held back by pruning. The many selections of *J. horizontalis* (creeping juniper) provide green and blue-gray spreading and cascading linear interest, and *J. squamata* 'Blue Star' slowly makes bright blue-gray, irregular mounds. The latter two combine nicely with other hardy woody plants in the same large pot.

- **Lonicera nitida**—While the plain green boxleaf honeysuckle makes a dense, fine-textured evergreen hedge in the open garden, 'Baggesen's Gold' commands attention in a pot with its long arching or cascading stems and yellow-gold foliage. Thin it out periodically to keep it in bounds, and try it in a fairly shady spot, where the foliage will glow a lively chartreuse.
- **Melianthus major**—Honeybush will captivate you with its blue-green, finely cut, complicated-looking large leaves on upright to sometimes floppy plants. Keep a small plant in a combination pot for its first year, but be prepared to isolate it in a large pot after that. It looks stunning with apricot, pink, or pale yellow, as well as with dark purple and even brown.
- **Phygelius**—When young and still small, the colorful flowers, arching lines, spacious form, and rather fine texture of Cape fuchsias combine and contrast appealingly with many plants. A more established pot of them can easily serve as a focal point. The large, elongated clusters of trumpetlike flowers

⑤ *Melianthus major,* the honeybush, cries out for use in containers, whether grown by itself or as a pale complement to vivid bloomers. Rangy older stems may need staking, but new shoots will soon emerge.

⑥ Many tubular-flowered triphylla-type fuchsias, like this *Fuchsia* 'Gartenmeister Bonstedt', tolerate heat far better than the more familiar-looking petticoatlike selections.

appear in shades of yellow, red, orange, and purple for most of the season.

- **Rosmarinus officinalis**—While I grow rosemary primarily for its dark green, fine-textured, needlelike foliage and supremely satisfying fragrance and flavor, I also enjoy the cheerful blue flowers indoors in late winter and sporadically outside in warmer weather. My favorites for containers are without question the weeping and prostrate selections, with their unpredictable but always interesting lines.

- **Salvia officinalis**—Don't make the mistake of relegating culinary sage to the inground herb garden. Every selection is container magic, including broader-leaved but still sagey gray-green 'Berggarten', yellow-edged 'Icterina', purple-infused 'Purpurascens', and 'Tricolor', edged in cream, pink, and purple. As a group, their mellow colors and medium-textured mounds combine with just about anything. Cut back severely in spring for dense mounds, or leave them alone to produce loose, open shapes full of character. Don't forget to give the leaves a rub every now and then.

- **Tetrapanax papyrifer**—Rice-paper plant cannot be mistaken for anything else: big, fanlike gray-green leaves appear on imposing, open, quite coarse but nevertheless supremely interesting plants. Grow a young one with fine-textured companions in a big pot, and then move it into its own pot as it expands with age.

7 No shrinking Violet here! *Tetrapanax papyrifera,* the rice-paper plant, makes a lasting impression even when just a few leaves high.

index

Thanks to Richard Hartlage for proposing the idea for this book and for providing his gorgeous photography to inspire me; Kate Rogers for keeping everything moving in the right direction; and Ingrid Emerick and Julie Van Pelt for making my words a suitable match for the photographs.

~ RR

Published in 2007 by
Timber Press, Inc.
The Haseltine Building
133 S.W. Second Avenue, Suite 450
Portland, Oregon 97204-3527, U.S.A.
www.timberpress.com

For contact information regarding editorial, marketing, sales,
and distribution in the United Kingdom, see www.timberpress.co.uk.

Reprinted in 2007

ISBN-13: 978-0-88192-834-1

Book design: Jane Jeszeck, www.jigsawseattle.com
Copy editor: Julie Van Pelt
Produced by Unleashed Book Development

A cross section of HLS color space (page 17) is reprinted under the terms
of the GNU Free Documentation License, Version 1.2 or any later version
published by the Free Software Foundation. The photograph of Sissinghurst
(page 80) is by Ray Rogers.

Miracle-Gro, Barad, Turface, and Peters are registered trademarks.

Printed in China

Catalog records for this book are available from the Library of Congress
and the British Library.